# Beyond the Familiar

*To Catherine, Alex, and Katy - PB*

*To Gill, Alice, and Emma - SM*

# Beyond the Familiar:

## Long-Term Growth through Customer Focus and Innovation

By Patrick Barwise

and Seán Meehan

This edition first published 2011


Under the Jossey-Bass imprint, Jossey-Bass, 989 Market Street, San Francisco CA 94103-1741, USA
www.jossey-bass.com

*Registered office*
John Wiley & Sons Ltd, The Atrium, Southern Gate, Chichester, West Sussex, PO19 8SQ, United Kingdom

For details of our global editorial offices, for customer services and for information about how to apply for permission to reuse the copyright material in this book please see our website at www.wiley.com.



*Library of Congress Cataloging-in-Publication Data*

Barwise, Patrick.
Beyond the familiar : long-term growth through customer focus and innovation / Patrick Barwise and Seán Meehan.
p. cm.
ISBN 978-0-470-97631-9
1. Customer services. 2. Success in business. I. Meehan, Seán. II. Title.
HF5415.5.B375 2011
658.8'12–dc22

2010050389

A catalogue record for this book is available from the British Library.

ISBN 978–0-470–97631–9 (hardback), ISBN 978–1-119-99380-3 (ebk)
ISBN 978–0-470-97650-0 (ebk), ISBN 978–0-470-97649-4 (ebk)

Set in 11/15 pt Garamond by Toppan Best-set Premedia Limited
Printed in Great Britain by TJ International Ltd, Padstow, Cornwall, UK

# Table of Contents

# Preface

Persistent growth is elusive. According to one estimate, during the 15-year period 1990–2004, only 24% of 6000 large public companies sustained profitable growth over any five consecutive years, only 5% over any ten consecutive years, and just 1% over the full 15 years.[1] Even the best companies lose the ability to generate long-term growth from time to time, in some cases irrecoverably. General Motors lost it in the 1970s, IBM in the 1980s, Motorola in the early 1990s, and Procter & Gamble in the late 1990s. GM and Motorola still haven't recovered.

Long-term growth results from driving the top line organically or through acquisitions, combined with good cost management. *Beyond the Familiar* focuses on organic growth, but also covers how to prioritize resource allocation and cost reduction. Many of the reasons why sustained profit growth is so hard to achieve are organizational: poor framing, fear, vested interests, complacency, and denial. In our research we have again and again seen how these block the free flow and discussion of the market information and ideas that power customer-focused execution and innovation and, ultimately, long-term growth.

***Open organization*** is, therefore, at the heart of our framework. It is *the* underlying imperative for firms aiming for long-term organic growth. It enables them to achieve the other four imperatives that directly drive revenue and profit:

- Offer and communicate a clear, relevant ***customer promise***
- Build ***customer trust*** and brand equity by reliably delivering that promise
- Drive the market by ***continuously improving*** the promise, while still reliably delivering it
- Get further ahead by occasionally ***innovating beyond the familiar***

For long-term success, you can't pick and choose from these imperatives. For instance, in the short term, innovating beyond the familiar is risky and may be optional, but in the long-term, failure to do so is riskier still and can even lead to extinction. At the same time, even a famously innovative company like Apple also needs to put a lot of unglamorous 'grunt work' into execution and incremental improvements, most of which never reaches the headlines. It is this hidden foundation that enables Apple and other long-term growth exemplars to innovate successfully 'beyond the familiar'.

Understanding customers' varying and evolving needs and preferences better than the competition is a recurrent theme of this book. Seeing the world through customers' eyes provides an unfamiliar, fresh and sometimes uncomfortable perspective that enables you to focus on what's actually most relevant to the market, rather than on what you just assume is most relevant.

In our earlier book *Simply Better: Winning and Keeping Customers by Delivering What Matters Most*,[2] we looked at 'differentiation that matters', that is, differentiation through the eyes of the customer. We argued that, despite marketers' obsession with uniqueness, what most customers want are products and services that just work, rather than offering unique features and benefits.

We build on this here by showing what managers need to do to ensure that valid, actionable customer insights are not only generated (from a wide range of sources, not just formal market research) but then reach those with the power to act on them and that they then do so. We see growth as an outcome, a consequence, of promising and consistently delivering better and better customer solutions and experiences. Further, we see this process as building a valuable long-term asset, the company's reputation in customers' minds (brand equity), which is then the platform for further growth.

To illustrate the framework, we have used a wide range of real-world cases of companies that have beaten the odds with sustained organic growth. Our examples aim to show the universality of the framework: they cover the spectrum from start up to mid cap and blue chip, both new and established markets, both B2B and B2C companies, and both products and services.

In summary, *Beyond the Familiar* offers a practical framework to help executives master the challenge of achieving long-term organic profit growth by **building strong brands based on actionable customer insights flowing freely through the business and ultimately leading to consistently great customer solutions and experiences.**

This is an optimistic book. It offers no single silver bullet but, true to its message, it has a clear customer promise – a strong one: *If you read this book and really apply the recommendations, you'll load the dice in favour of your business's likelihood of delivering long-term, market-driving organic profit growth.*

# Acknowledgements

*Beyond the Familiar* would never have seen the light of day without the help of many people. We wish to offer a special 'thank you' to a few in particular.

This is a practical book for practical managers, so the case studies play a central role. We use them to illustrate the ideas, bring them to life and - we hope - encourage you to emulate the most successful and learn from the mistakes of the less successful. Much of the material comes from public sources but we are also greatly indebted to the many executives who have generously provided unpublished data and personal insights on their companies or former companies. A few have requested anonymity but, among those who have not, we would especially like to thank Chris Havemann (Research Now), Simon Lyons, Bruce Pool and Rupert Soames (Aggreko), Carol Berning, Peter Carter, Werner Geissler and Scott Stewart (P&G), Wanda Pogue (Saatchi & Saatchi), Fergus Boyd (Virgin Atlantic), Steve Liguori and Anubhav Ranjan (GE), Kris Gopalakrishnan, Bikramjit Maitra, Aditya Nath Jha, Nandan Nilekani, and Sanjay Purohit (Infosys), and Geert van Kuyck (Philips).

We also draw on a wide range of academic research, listed in the reference notes at the back. As well as this formally cited literature, however, over the five years it has taken us to research and write this book, we have greatly benefited from countless informal discussions with our academic colleagues at London Business

School and IMD, a constant source of ideas, tough questions, and encouragement, as well as from the generous research support of the Centre for Marketing at LBS and the Global Research Fund at IMD.

Next, we would like to thank our four outstanding researchers Emma Macdonald, Willem Smit, Mandeep Waraich, and Sandeep Waraich. They all went way beyond the brief, adding new ideas and suggestions and providing constructive challenge at every stage. Their excellent work has contributed greatly to the quality of the case studies, the breadth of the academic research base, and the tightness of the argument.

The book has also benefited from conversations with, and feedback from, a range of other people. Among scholars at other business schools, we would specifically like to thank George Day (Wharton), Liz Morrison (NYU), Eric Von Hippel (MIT), and Gerald Zaltman (HBS). Our understanding of the practicalities of customer satisfaction - and dissatisfaction - metrics was much helped by talking to Fred Reichheld (Bain) and Claes Fornell, David Ham, and Sheri Teodoru (CFI Group). Tania Dussey-Cavassini, John Evans, Loic Frank, Stefan Michel, Jim Pulcrano and Stuart Read provided particularly creative suggestions along the way. Tim Ambler, Alex Barwise, Charlie Dawson, Bill Fischer, Kit Harman, Bernie Jaworski, Nancy Lowd, Jean-Louis Rufener, Kirsten Sandberg, Chris Styles, and Peter Vicary-Smith all provided helpful comments on the various drafts. We also benefited from the detailed reviews and professional expertise of our editorial consultant Morgen Witzel. Thanks also to Rosemary Nixon and all the team at John Wiley/ Jossey-Bass for efficiently bringing our manuscript to you the reader.

Our final thank you is to those who, day in and day out, have provided essential administrative back up and support, especially Laura Hall, Sylvie Happe, Maryline Mermillod, and Margaret Walls.

# CHAPTER ONE

# WHAT EVERY CEO WANTS

*'Organic growth is always stronger'*
– Sir Martin Sorrell, Chief Executive, WPP Group[3]

Every CEO wants **sustained, profitable, organic growth**. Even firms that grow mainly by acquisition – with its high failure rate – usually need to show that they can increase value through top-line growth of the combined business as well as through cost-cutting. Organic growth therefore lies at the heart of long-term shareholder value creation for almost all businesses.

We all know of companies like Procter & Gamble, Apple, Canon, IBM, Infosys, BestBuy, Oticon and Zara that seem to achieve this kind of profitable organic growth year after year. They go from strength to strength, from success to success. How do they do it?

Each has a different strategy and business model, but ultimately, they all succeed because they do a few obvious, fundamental things well, and they do them over and over again. Firms that achieve sustained, profitable organic growth have an ***open organization*** at their core. They exploit the critical advantages this brings to achieve four key imperatives:

- Offer and communicate a clear, relevant ***customer promise***.
- Build ***customer trust*** and brand equity by reliably delivering that promise

- Drive the market by ***continuously improving*** the promise, while still reliably delivering it
- Get further ahead by occasionally ***innovating beyond the familiar***

Although these ideas are familiar to everyone, putting them into practice is extremely difficult, which is why so few firms manage to deliver lasting organic profit growth. To hit the sweet spot, you need to get all of this right and in balance, as illustrated in the framework for this book (Figure 1.1).

Applying this framework requires firms to overcome a number of challenges. They must be more adept than their competitors at keeping in touch with customers' needs - much easier to say than to do. They must overcome the tensions between the pressure for short-term profits (especially through cost-cutting) and the need to build long-term customer and shareholder value. They must tackle organizational arrogance, complacency, denial, boredom, and the tendency to get distracted by what's new and exciting instead of what's important. Worst of all - especially with today's higher unemployment - they must reduce the corrosive, unacknowledged

Figure 1.1: The Organic Growth Framework

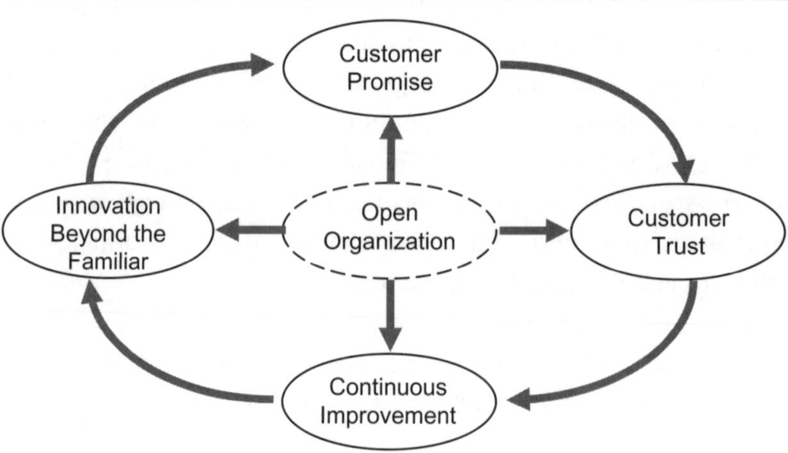

influence of fear, or at least deference, within the organization which prevents the open communication required to enable customer-focused improvement and innovation.

To introduce the issues, we first look at the twists and turns that have characterized the global market for mobile phone handsets since it came of age in the 1990s. There are many lessons to be drawn from the contrasting approaches and performance of Motorola and Nokia up to the launch of the Apple iPhone in 1997. Since then, the further lesson is how Nokia's winning formula has, so far, fallen short in the new market conditions created by Apple and now Google. This case shows how achieving organic growth is a never-ending challenge. No-one knows which firm will enjoy most success over the coming years, but the winners will be those that successfully drive the market through relentless customer focus combined with innovation beyond the familiar.

## Global Mobile Phone Handsets: How Nokia Toppled Motorola only to Lose its Way

In April 1994, *Fortune* quoted a vice president of research at consulting firm AT Kearney as saying, *'Motorola is the best-managed company in the world. Nobody else is even close'*. *Fortune* described Motorola as a leader in innovation, total quality management (TQM), business process engineering, training, teamwork, and empowerment, and praised its '... *candid internal debate that remains rare in corporate America*'. In a shaky financial market, Motorola's stock was trading at an all-time high, driven by record sales and profits.[4]

Motorola's flagship business was its market-leading cell phone division, with a global market share in 1994 of 45%, more than twice the 20% share of its closest competitor, Finland's Nokia. But by 2000, all this had changed. Nokia was the clear market leader with a global share of 31%, while Motorola's had collapsed to just

15%.[5] Since then, Motorola's problem-ridden handset business has suffered numerous losses, redundancies, new leaders, and strategy re-launches.[6] There was a false dawn in 2004–6, driven by the success of the attractive RAZR phone, but by Q2 2010 Motorola's market share had fallen to an all-time low of 2.8%, well behind Samsung's 20.1%, LG's 9%, and RIM and Sony Ericsson's 3.4% each. Nokia, despite its poor performance in the high-growth smart phone segment, remained clear market leader with a 34.2% global market share.[7]

How did a market leader described as the *'best-managed company in the world'* stumble so badly, not just once, but again and again, while an obscure Finnish company left it for dust? While Nokia now faces serious challenges, which we'll discuss, it achieved market leadership by being *consistently* better managed than Motorola for over 15 years.

### *Contrasting Growth Strategies*

In the late 1980s, Nokia was a highly-diversified manufacturing company known more for its rubber boots than its fledgling telecom network and handsets business.[8] In May 1992, it decided to focus primarily on capturing the growth potential of consumer mobile telephones. In 1996 CEO, Jorma Olilla, wrote to shareholders:

> 'Focus on the telecommunications industry means several things to us. First, it means the need to continue to enhance the existing competence base of the company. Second, it means a necessity to watch constantly for new opportunities in areas related to our main operations. Third, it means a firm commitment to achieve operational excellence within the company through improved business processes. ... Thanks to our single-minded telecommunications orientation, we can now meet customer needs, technological as well as marketing challenges with the full strength of our organization.'[9]

In sharp contrast, by the early 1990s, Motorola was designing, manufacturing, and distributing a huge range of electronic products: semiconductors, cell phones and cellular infrastructure, computers, two-way radio products and systems, pagers, wireless and wire line data communications systems and services, satellite communication systems, and electronic control systems.

Motorola had a complex organization in which each business had wide autonomy, all under a general belief that computing and communications were converging and creating exciting but unpredictable opportunities and, presumably, that Motorola should aim to be in touch with as many of the relevant technologies and trends as possible: in 1995, it generated over 1000 patents. It became more complex and diversified as it grew through major investments (for example Iridium[10], a $5bn ultra high-tech system of privately owned satellites) and acquisitions (the $17bn acquisition of General Instrument, the USA's largest producer of cable TV set top boxes).

The advantage of Nokia's greater focus becomes clearer when we examine the companies' contrasting approaches to execution. For nearly 20 years, Nokia addressed *all* the requirements of our organic growth framework with greater consistency than most of its competitors, especially Motorola.

### *'Offer and communicate a clear, relevant customer promise'*

In 1991, Nokia was among the first firms to see that digital technology would transform the mobile phone market from a limited application for a privileged few into a huge and fast-growing mass market. To succeed, it would need to make the Nokia brand a household name. It hired Anssi Vanjoki, a young 3M marketer, to lead its brand strategy. Anssi argued that the best companies thought about the brand in every aspect of the value chain – product design, production, distribution, and service – as well as advertising and promotion. Nokia therefore adopted a holistic brand approach covering everything which directly or indirectly impacted its customers (mobile operators) and consumers, including internal functions such as HR and finance.

Nokia, initially unknown among consumers outside Finland, spent almost $1 billion on brand communications through the 1990s. It eschewed promoting technical features and stressed emotional benefits such as inspired technology, ease of use, and durability. Since 1992, it has used the English-language slogan, *'Connecting people'* globally.[11] With a discipline sadly lacking in many global consumer businesses, the look and feel of Nokia products was the same everywhere. In developing markets, Nokia's regional leaders had wide autonomy, but the blue logo, the ring tone, and the *'Connecting people'* tagline were mandatory. Amazingly, by 2000, Nokia was the world's fifth most valuable brand, according to Interbrand.[12]

Motorola, too, had been primarily a business-to-business (B2B) brand in the early 1990s. Once it started mass producing cell phones, its consumer brand awareness grew quickly due to its wide distribution and exposure. However, it was slow to recognise the need for a clear, consistent, consumer-relevant brand promise. This lack of clarity and consistency is reflected in its numerous short-lived brand slogans:

- *'What you never thought possible' [1996–2000]*
- *'Intelligence Everywhere' [2000–2004]*
- *'Seamless Mobility' [2004]*
- *'Mobile Me' [2005]*
- *'Hello Moto' [2006–2008]*
- *'We Generation' [2008]*

### *'Build customer trust and brand equity by reliably delivering on that promise'*

Nokia worked hard to deliver on its brand promise. In fact promise-keeping – 'customer commitment' – to trade customers and consumers has been an explicit part of its strategy since 1992. Motorola never quite grasped the critical importance of reliably delivering the customer promise. In 1995, Ameritech - a key customer - told Motorola it would need digital handsets in one year. Two years later Ameritech was still waiting and reluctantly went elsewhere. At the consumer level, Motorola's beautifully designed RAZR phone was a big hit in 2004–06. But this success was not maintained because, although consumers loved the design, they found the user interface slow and difficult. Ease of use is crucial in this market - the RAZR failed to deliver it.

In case this sounds easy, Nokia too had challenges. When booming global sales growth unexpectedly declined in late 1995, it experienced a rapid inventory build up. The ensuing alarm was such that Nokia saw its share price halve between September 1995 and February 1996.[13] Recognizing that *'The mobile phone business amounts to a large-scale logistical exercise'*,[14] it reorganized its supply chain and averted a lasting crisis. By the end of 1996, Nokia had regained its strong number two global position and was already the market leader in the fast-growing digital handset category.

Motorola, which 20 years ago had a strong, well-established brand, failed to build on its head start: it didn't focus sufficiently on promising and consistently delivering a complete customer-relevant offer - product, delivery, and service. Nokia's subsequent success, in contrast, was based on building a well-known brand trusted by both mobile operators and consumers.

### *'Drive the market by continuously improving on that promise, while still reliably delivering it'*

Like most companies, both Motorola and Nokia were heavily committed to innovation as a core source of competitive advantage. But their approaches could hardly be more different.

Nokia was the first supplier to sell phones that work on every major cellular standard and, as already discussed, the first to recognize the importance of supply chain management. It was also the first to target the whole of the global 'income pyramid', aiming to reach the four billion people still unconnected as well as the minority who were already connected. Of course, Nokia has also been the first to introduce many product improvements, but these have usually been incremental, such as the first mobile handset with an integrated FM radio, games and a calendar. Despite Nokia's brave decision to focus solely on telecommunications, *breakthrough* product innovation is not part of its DNA.

In sharp contrast, Motorola was a serial breakthrough technology player. It developed the world's first:

- Commercial cell phone (1983)
- Working prototype of a GSM cellular system and phones (1991)
- Two-way pager (1995)
- GPRS cellular system (2000)
- 3G nationwide network (Japan) (2002)[15]

To Motorola, innovation mainly meant being the first to introduce a heroic, blockbuster, new product. To Nokia, the main emphasis was improving the delivery of the promise through a series of incremental products and process innovations. This difference in emphasis was wryly noted by Tom Meredith, Motorola's embattled CFO, in 2007:

> 'Motorola's history is anything but boring, littered with iconic phones from the StarTec to the recent hit with the RAZR. But you'd be hard pressed to name an iconic product from market leader Nokia.'[16]

As Jack Johnson [name disguised], a former Motorola executive told us, *'Nokia started with consumer insights. It observed consumers and learned anthropologically and sociologically about how people live, then tried to humbly serve them up with solu-*

*tions. Motorola's approach was: let's see what the promise of technology can unleash'.*

### *'Get further ahead by occasionally innovating beyond the familiar'*

Of the five elements in the framework, this is the one where Nokia is weakest, although even here, its track record may be stronger than many people realize. As we've discussed, in 1992 it took a brave decision to focus entirely on telecommunications. Nokia was also one of the main innovators driving the switch from analog to digital mobile telephony. Both its branding strategy and its emphasis on supply chain management took it into territory unfamiliar to both itself and the industry. But, as we've noted, in the enhancement and execution of its customer promise its main emphasis has been on incremental not radical innovation. It now faces serious competition in the smart-phone segment from new entrants including Apple, a world leader in innovating beyond the familiar.

Given Motorola's emphasis on looking for the next big thing, one might expect it to be stronger than Nokia on breakthrough innovation, but – in mobile handsets – it hasn't been. Motorola was slow to spot the switch from analog to digital and, at least with hindsight, its investment in the satellite-based Iridium was a disaster. Nor does Motorola's preference for breakthrough over incremental innovation leave it any better placed than Nokia to compete against Apple, Google, and Blackberry (RIM) in the fast-changing smart-phone market.

### *'Put an Open Organization at the Core'*

Nokia has always been ambitious. It set out to be the global handset market leader (achieved 1998), to lead by 1.5 times (achieved 2000), to be a leading consumer brand (Top 5 global brand according to Interbrand in 2000), and to be best at supply chain management (#1 in 2007 according to AMR).[17]

Nokia has also always been a humble company. Its four values, defined by employees, *'Very Human, Engaging You, Passion for Innovation,* and *Working Together'* are tied together via the deep-rooted Finnish character of *'Noyryys',* meaning humility.[18]

There are conflicting views about Motorola's culture. Its handset business has been described on the one hand as epitomizing the values of a market-oriented firm (collaboration, respect, keeping promises, empathy, trust)[19] and on the other as 'bureaucratic', 'back-stabbing', 'toxic', and 'resulting in wasted effort'.[20]

Many would argue that, at a crucial period of great change in the market, Motorola's leadership lived in a different world from the rest of the organization. While top managers were saying the right things about delivering leading edge solutions, the reality of everyday experience for employees and customers was quite different.[21] A former executive described bureaucracy running amok: *'The last year I was there, you could get nothing accomplished. The whole organization was in paralysis. ... You couldn't make a decision without needing 99 other people to make a decision. It was horrible'*. She didn't blame Galvin for creating the problems but said: *'He was asleep at the switch while some of his lieutenants screwed up'.*[22]

Out-of-touch leadership and poor strategy might help explain Motorola's poor execution and inability to deliver on its promises. Once the company became embroiled in these problems, effective execution is likely to have become harder and harder, creating a vicious circle of falling behind the market, losing money, having to cancel projects and lose more staff, and so on.

A benefit Nokia enjoyed from its openness was enhanced responsiveness. For example, around 2003, it was developing a reputation amongst carriers that: *'Nokia means "No"'*. In response, it re-structured the organization and introduced sophisticated global consumer segmentation. These actions were designed to ensure that it continued to be in touch with its customers and consumers and responsive to their needs. In 2007, however, Nokia was hit by a disruptive new competitor, Apple.

## After the iPhone: Has Nokia Lost It?

The Apple iPhone was launched in summer 2007. An immediate hit, it had dramatic consequences for the handset industry. Nokia's inability to field a credible response has precipitated a freefall in its margins and share price. This collapse need never have happened. Some claim that over time Nokia lost touch with the market, so that in 2004 it even rejected a proposal to develop a Nokia online applications store. It has certainly been slow to improve the Symbian operating system - a requirement if it is to develop a fully competitive smart phone. Reminiscent of former rival Motorola, employees now talk of bureaucracy and infighting.[23] The departure, announced in September 2010, of CEO Olli-Pekka Kallavuso, Anssi Vanjoki (by then head of mobile solutions), and chairman Jorma Ollila suggests that the company accepts the need to turn a page. As Jack Johnson opines, Nokia needs to be bold and move fast, otherwise it may end up like Motorola:

> 'The last thing Nokia needs right now is to be incrementalist, because the world is changing again. Nokia today is where Motorola was in 1994 - not for the same reasons, but just as exposed'.

The challenge is not just that the pace of handset innovation has accelerated, it is that Nokia is primarily a hardware manufacturer with roots in mobile telephony while the iPhone is a powerful handheld computer and part of an ecosystem including software, mobile internet, and a huge range of applications. To-date, this has proved too far 'beyond the familiar' for Nokia. Even its hitherto very successful brand promise - connecting people - is no longer adequate.

Further, both Nokia and Apple are now under pressure from other handset manufacturers using Google's Android operating system. At the time of writing (September 2010) these other competitors, in combination, are outpacing both Apple and Nokia in the smart phone market, threatening to make Android the standard for application developers, network operators, and consumers. Nokia's

Symbian operating system might become a historical relic unless it can quickly improve its user interface and portfolio of applications, both areas where Apple has dramatically raised the bar.

Nokia's urgent challenge is to execute its strategy to be the global mass market enabler of mobile internet solutions while still exploiting its many continuing competitive advantages: handset design, supply chain and production; strong global brand, distribution and customer base; and leadership in many of the highest growth markets in the world (India, parts of Africa) where Apple is not meaningfully present and Nokia is preferred to HTC and other Android handset brands.

It is much too early to write Nokia off as a significant player in the global mobile handset market. Who is to say it cannot re-emerge from crisis, just as Apple did after two near-death experiences, as we'll discuss in Chapter 5.[24] What we can say is that Motorola – the clear market leader 15 years ago – is low on the list of Nokia's strategic concerns. Motorola is not even at the races, because of its persistent failure to offer and communicate a clear, relevant customer promise, build trust and brand equity by reliably delivering on that promise, drive the market through continuous improvements, and create an open, customer-focused organization. Innovation beyond the familiar is a requirement for long-term organic profit growth – but so are all the other elements in the organic growth framework in Figure 1.1. This framework provides the main structure for the book, a chapter for each of the five elements.

## Three Recurrent Themes

In addition to the five elements of the framework, there are three other themes which recur throughout the book:

- Brand equity and customer experience
- Customer focus and insights

- Continuous improvement versus 'heroic' breakthrough innovation.

## Brand Equity and Customer Experience

When we say 'brand' in this book, we mean 'brand equity', that is, customers' and prospects' beliefs and expectations about products and services sold under the brand name, and about the company that sells them. Brand equity matters because it can significantly increase customers' likelihood of choosing, and the price they are willing to pay for, products and services sold under the associated brand name. Further, because it resides in customers' long-term memory, it can have a long-term impact on business performance.

As we saw with Nokia, great brands are built holistically by reliably delivering a relevant customer experience, reinforced by communications – not the other way round. If great brands like American Express, Apple, Disney, GE, Google, HSBC, IBM, Mercedes-Benz, PwC, Shell, Singapore Airlines, and Tide started letting their customers down, they wouldn't be able recover through brilliant advertising. Concretely, who would seriously propose that advertising alone would have solved Toyota's recent sudden acceleration crisis?

Brand equity acts as a flywheel: customers' previous experience (and the experience-based recommendations of others they trust – close friends and colleagues, trusted third parties) encourages them to keep buying, and themselves recommending, the brand over time. In fact, a strong brand is remarkably hard to destroy: customers who have a bad experience with the brand assume it's a one-off until the negative evidence becomes hard to deny.

## Customer Focus and Insights

The second recurring theme is customer focus and insights. As well as wanting the company to be more innovative, most CEOs also want their businesses to be more customer-focused.

'Customer-focused' doesn't mean 'customer-driven', either. Improvement and innovation have to be driven by people inside the organization. This includes not only senior managers but also everyone from the call center operator who suggests a better way of classifying customer questions through to entrepreneurs like Fred Smith at Fedex or Ikea's Ingvar Kamprad, with a vision of a much better way of serving customers.

Companies can never be completely customer-driven because:

- Companies can't afford to give all customers what they want at a price they're willing to pay. They have to prioritize.
- Customers often don't know what they want until someone offers it and they try it.

The most successful companies continuously raise customers' expectations above what they are used to (and the competition can deliver) while still - crucially - ensuring reliable execution to meet the customers' newly raised expectations. This approach is customer-focused, not customer-driven. It is difficult because:

- The aim must be not just to meet customer needs but to do so profitably, which means that there is a relentless pressure on costs. There is often tension between cost management and customer satisfaction.
- Valid and actionable customer insights are elusive, especially in areas where the customers themselves don't know what they want. Our advice is to use the full range of sources of insight, from formal market research to 'immersive' customer contacts and sophisticated database analysis.
- Valid, actionable customer insights are worthless unless they reach those with the power to act on them and they then do so. For this to happen, the message needs to be communicated up the hierarchy and be accepted and exploited, leading to an appropriate response. This applies whether the idea for an innovation comes from a new market

insight, a new technology, or anywhere else. In fact, some of the worst cases of fear stifling open discussion happen when the proposed innovation comes from the top.
- Irrelevant attempts to be different from the competition distract firms from delivering what matters most to current and prospective customers.

## Continuous Improvement versus Heroic Breakthrough Innovation

Everyone agrees that the key driver of sustained, market-driving organic growth is, in some sense, innovation. But a high proportion of innovations fail - estimates range from 40–95% depending on the definition[25] - and there is a lot of confusion around the topic. The high failure rate and confusion are not due to lack of attention. The business shelves of bookstores are groaning under the weight of books on innovation. As we see it, there are two big problems with most of these books: their obsession with heroic breakthrough innovation and their failure to show how to keep innovation customer-relevant.

In *Animal Farm*, George Orwell's satire on the Soviet Union under Stalin, policy was boiled down to a slogan so simple that even the chickens could understand it: *'Four legs good, two legs bad'*.[26] To be fair, books on innovation implicitly assume managers are twice as smart as the chickens in *Animal Farm* and can cope with not one but two messages (although they rarely distinguish clearly between them):

- *'Radical good, incremental bad'*: the first assumption is that you should prioritize bold, disruptive innovations which lead to a quantum improvement in product, service, business systems, or value for money.
- *'Pioneer good, follower bad'*: the second assumption is that you should always aim to be the first to introduce an innovation.

According to this conventional wisdom, the ideal therefore is what we're calling 'heroic breakthrough' innovation which is *both radical and pioneering*, ie:

- The innovation is a big step, not just an incremental improvement and
- The firm is the first competitor to introduce it.

Successful heroic breakthrough innovations are highly profitable and generate a lot of ego-boosting publicity for the innovators. The media love these stories and companies that are first to the market with a genuine - or even just plausible - breakthrough innovation are guaranteed a lot of coverage. But the siren call of publicity should not distract you from the fact that heroic breakthrough innovations are expensive and usually fail.

Around 1440, Johannes Gutenberg introduced to Europe the movable-type printing press, an archetypal breakthrough innovation. Within a few years he was bankrupt. Advantage went to the 'fast followers' like the Englishman William Caxton, who took Gutenberg's innovation and used it to get rich. Today, as we discuss in Chapter 5, many highly successful firms have never made a heroic breakthrough innovation. They are often 'fast followers', capitalizing on ideas generated by others at great risk and cost.[27]

If you take one idea away from this book, it should be that **the starting point for long-term, market-leading organic profit growth is to deliver the main current category benefits to your existing customers better than the competition**. This is the exact opposite of the frequent and popular recommendation to start by looking for heroic breakthrough innovations. It is not an argument for stopping at that point - the book is called *Beyond the Familiar* not *Stick to What You Know* - but the starting point is, so to speak, inside the box.

A related theme is the complex relationship between innovation and customer focus. This is not just a matter of listening to customers and then creating new products or services in response to what they tell you. That is part of it, but not the whole picture. Although customer insights are crucial, rather than being merely (or often) the starting point, their relationship with innovation goes both ways and relates to all stages of the process, from generating and selecting the initial idea, through development, piloting/prototyping and further development, launch, and longer-term continuous improvement. At each stage, those driving the innovation need to keep checking their emerging ideas and proposals against potential customers. At the same time, new or unexpected customer insights can suggest entirely new ideas or changes to existing ones.

## Conclusion: The Structure of the Book and Five Killer Questions

The other main chapters cover the five elements in the framework one by one:

- Your promise to the customer (Chapter 2)
- Delivering today's promise better and better every day (Chapter 3)
- Driving the market by relentlessly improving the promise (Chapter 4)
- Innovating beyond the familiar (Chapter 5)
- Opening up: what leaders must do (Chapter 6)

To conclude this chapter, we offer five killer questions which every leader should ask. Each corresponds to one of the five elements in the framework and we'll return to it as part of the relevant chapter. Of course, for each element, there are many other questions you could and should ask, but these five should help you see the potential for improvement, and where the biggest opportunities are likely to be:[28]

- *Can your middle managers accurately describe your customer promise?*
- *Can all members of your senior executive team name the three things that most undermine trust among your existing customers?*
- *Is your brand really the best option for customers? Will it continue to be next month and next year?*
- *Have you embraced any novel ideas that have produced significant innovations beyond the familiar during the past year?*
- *Have front-line staff asked you any uncomfortable questions or suggested any important improvements to your offering during the last three months?*

If you believe the answer to all five questions is yes, there are two possibilities. One is that you're right, in which case the prospects for your company are brilliant and you don't have much to learn from this book. Alternatively, you're mistaken, in which case you're also unlikely to learn much from the book unless you do something technically easy but emotionally difficult, which is to gather objective evidence on each question.

For instance, you may think that your middle managers can accurately describe your customer promise (and they probably think so too) but have you asked them? Are their answers concise, consistent, convincing, and correct? If so, bravo! - your organization is in the small, excellent minority on this dimension. If, more likely, the honest answer is no, you've already identified an area for improvement. The same applies for all five elements of the framework.

We now turn to the first of these, how to offer and communicate a clear, relevant customer promise.

## Chapter Two

# Your Promise to the Customer

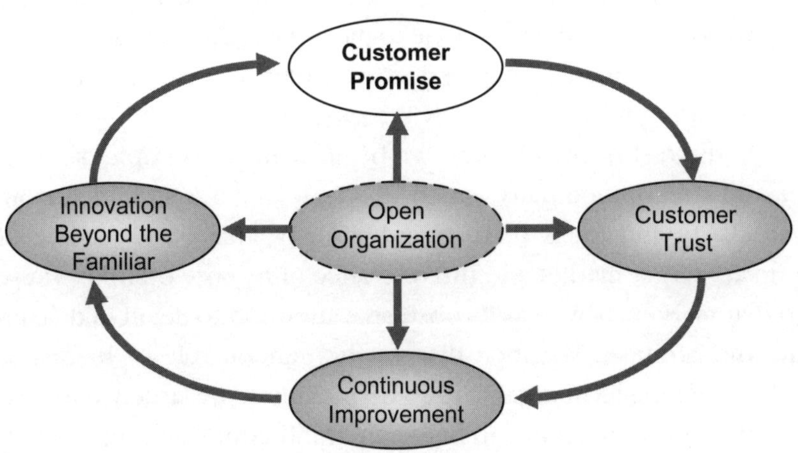


*'Customers must recognize that you stand for something.'*
- Howard Schultz, Founder of Starbucks.[29]

The first step on the road to sustainable profit growth is to have a clear brand strategy that tells you, your people, and your customers two things: who you are aiming to serve and what you are promising to do for them. Obviously, you need to ensure that this core promise is successfully communicated to customers and potential customers so that they know what benefits to expect if they buy your product or service. What may be less obvious is the extent to which you also need to communicate it throughout your company, at all levels and across all functions. Ideally, everyone in the company should understand who the target customers are and what the core brand promise is. It tells them what to prioritize and thus guides daily decision making. That's why the diagnostic question for this chapter focuses on middle managers:

**'Can your middle managers accurately describe your customer promise?'**

If your middle managers understand the brand promise, the chances are much higher that they and others further down the line will aim to do what needs to be done to meet the right customer expectations; if the middle managers don't really know the brand promise, there's little chance that this will happen.

In the rest of the chapter, we begin with an example of a successful start-up company, much of whose success stemmed from the clarity and focus of its brand strategy, that is, its choice of primary target market and the relevance of its core brand promise to that market, as well as its obsessive attention to detail in delivering the promise. We then discuss the generic role of brands as drivers of long-term organic growth, including the largely unrecognized two-way relationship between brand equity and innovation, and the value of brands in helping the business survive shocks and missteps.

This raises the crucial practical question of how to build and maintain a valuable brand. We describe this as the ART of brand-building, where ART stands for *awareness, relevance,* and *trust*, the three things all valuable brands have in common, however much they vary in other ways. We discuss how to achieve the first two of these, awareness and relevance - trust being the topic of Chapter 3.

## How *Research Now* Stood and Delivered

In April 2000 - just as the technology bubble started to collapse - Chris Havemann and Andrew Cooper set up The Mobile Channel

(TMC), aiming to become the UK's number one platform for permission-based mobile advertising using SMS text messaging. After a successful concept test,[30] TMC obtained angel funding in early 2001, despite the difficult financial climate. Mobile marketing took much longer to develop than expected, however, and the business lacked sufficient capital to build a consumer database large enough to be useful for advertising purposes beyond small-scale trials of the new medium.

By early 2003, TMC's database comprised around 100,000 people, mainly hard-to-reach teenagers and young adults. Most of these names had been acquired at low cost from financially distressed internet start-ups. For each name, TMC had a mobile phone number, an email address, some data on demographics and interests, and permission to send up to five commercial text messages per day for an incentive of five pence per message (equivalent to about eight US cents). It had also built up some less tangible assets: nearly three years' hard experience of operating on a shoestring in the marketing services market right through an advertising recession; relationships with major clients such as Johnson & Johnson and Diageo, and their agencies; and above all, a reputation among these blue-chip clients for straight, honest dealing, excellent service, and value for money. Nevertheless, the business was not viable. There simply was not enough money coming in to cover TMC's costs, although these had been pared right back. There was little prospect of profits before the funding ran out.

### *The switch to Research Now*

The breakthrough came in summer 2003. Two clients, Procter & Gamble and Panasonic, had each asked TMC not only to run another small-scale mobile advertising campaign but also to do some follow-up research on its impact, using an email survey. Chris and Andrew suddenly realized that, although a panel of 100,000 young consumers was too small for mainstream advertising purposes, it was easily big enough for market research purposes. Online market research was taking off in a big way in North America but was much less developed elsewhere, where internet penetration was lower and the research market more geographically fragmented. Online fieldwork is both cheaper and faster than traditional methods using telephone or face-to-face interviews, while providing equally good or better data if well managed. Growth prospects were therefore excellent.

Chris and Andrew switched to an ambitious new, single-minded objective: to turn TMC into Europe's leading specialist in online market research fieldwork. They chose Research Now (RN) as the new corporate brand and Valued Opinions (and foreign language equivalents) as the consumer brand for panellists. The RN brand promise was simple: *High-quality online survey data, on time and on budget.*

The main competitors were either companies set up by large market research and marketing services groups such as Lightspeed (WPP) or pure play early movers such as Greenfield Online (US) and Ciao (Italy). Another was the UK company YouGov, initially specializing in surveys for government departments and the media. RN therefore decided to target other market research firms, especially those large enough to work with blue-chip clients but not large enough to justify the cost of building and maintaining their own online panels. RN would continue to work directly with some major corporate clients and opportunistically for other companies such as management consultants, PR companies, hedge funds, and even competitor research agencies if the RN panel happened to fill a gap in the competitor's coverage. The brand promise - high-quality online survey data, on time and on budget - was highly relevant to all of these segments.

The rest is history. RN launched in November 2003. Its turnover grew tenfold from £240 thousand for the six months to April 2004 to £2.4 million for the six months to October 2005. By then it had 700,000 panellists in eight countries and 46 employees in three countries. It was making an operating profit of 14% of revenue and had just (August 2005) floated on Aim, the London

Stock Exchange junior market. In February 2007, it acquired OpenVenue, the top online fieldwork company in Canada, with a similar commitment to data quality and client service and significant US sales. By then, RN already had offices in New York, Chicago and San Francisco, but the OpenVenue acquisition took it straight to being the 5th biggest online fieldwork company in North America.

Despite some setbacks, including a profit warning in 2007 due to an earlier accounting error, the organic growth of the merged company continued apace and in December 2009, RN was acquired for £85 million by Dallas-based e-Rewards, the world's largest by invitation only online research panel. From its August 2005 flotation to its acquisition by e-Rewards, RN was the highest-performing media stock in Europe (having already generated an even higher ROI for the stage 1 investors who cashed out at the flotation).[31] Chris Havemann was appointed CEO of e-Rewards. Earlier that year, he had won the Aim UK Entrepreneur of the Year award. Andrew Cooper, the other co-founder, had stayed with RN as Managing Director through the bad times but then left in 2008 to set up another new business, Verve, a specialist in online customer advisory panels and brand communities.

### *The RN brand promise*

The core RN brand promise - ***high-quality online data, on time and on budget*** - is simple. RN also provides outstanding client service as well as tools to help clients collect and analyze the data (sample design, scripting, online reporting, analytical tools, staff training, etc) but it does not aim or claim to interpret the results or spell out their implications. This is consistent with its target market being market research agencies and sophisticated corporate clients with detailed knowledge of their industries: both these segments know how to design research studies and interpret and exploit data. RN therefore aims to be the world's best online *fieldwork* agency, not a full-service online market research agency. It does not compete against its agency clients. Similarly, it uses extensive proprietary software but is not a technology company. Good strategy is usually as much about whom you don't target and what you don't promise as about whom and what you do target and promise.

### *The Valued Opinions brand promise*

RN's ability to deliver its brand promise to clients itself depends on the strength of the Valued Opinions brand among panellists, especially in terms of panellist retention. The main Valued Opinions brand promise is simply that *someone is interested in what you think*. Panellists are also paid a small incentive as a way of saying thank you, and given feedback on how their responses differ from those of others. RN works hard to make the panellist experience interesting (through accurate profiling and targeting), enjoyable (increasingly using rich media stimuli) and straightforward (a user-friendly interface). Despite all the excitement about social media, it is cautious about adding a community dimension, since for most surveys the aim is to avoid panellists influencing each other's responses.

## The Brand as a Flywheel of Organic Growth

Research Now illustrates some generic issues to which we now turn, starting with the value of a strong brand based on a clear definition of the target market, high brand awareness within that market, a brand promise relevant to the market, and the kind of trust that has to be earned the hard way. These are essential foundations for long-term, market-leading organic profit growth, which *always* comes from developing and consistently delivering a relevant promise to customers. It takes time and energy to build a valuable brand, but once established, it has a big role in maintaining the direction and momentum of the business.

The last 20 years have seen a great increase in research on brands and the growth of specialist brand consultancies. At the same time, brands have also become a source of much hype, jargon, and confusion. Even today, when people hear the word *'brand'*, they tend to think mainly of *'branding'*, that is, the brand name, logo, advertising, and so on. Many people in business-to-business (B2B) or service markets still think that brands are relevant only in consumer product markets, although they would all agree that a company's reputation and credibility in the market are crucial, which is just a looser way of describing the brand.

In fact, there's a close chicken-and-egg relationship between brand and long-term organic profit growth, as we'll explain, but you'd never guess this from most of the literature: few books on the issues discussed in *Beyond The Familiar* (execution, customer-focused innovation, organizational values, organic growth) even mention brands, while conversely, few books on brands say much about these other issues.

This confusion partly arises because the word *brand*, as a noun, can validly be used to mean at least three categorically different things[32]:

- **A named product or service** (as in *"Which brand did you buy?"*)
- **A trademark** (as in *"Under which brand* [i.e. name] *shall we sell this new product?"*)
- **Brand equity** (as in *"Will this new product extension strengthen or dilute the brand?"*).

No wonder, in the words of Jeremy Bullmore, a member of the WPP advisory board, '*When CEOs try to think about brands, their brains hurt*'.[33]

**When we say 'brand' in this book, we mean brand equity.** This refers to customers' and prospects' beliefs and expectations about products and services sold under a specific trademark, and about the company that sells them. Because brand equity exists in customers' long-term memory, it can have very long-term value for the company: the 50-year-old man still using the same bank as his parents, or fulfilling a lifelong dream by buying a Jaguar or Mercedes, is partly acting on brand impressions first acquired in childhood - and may even pass a similar desire for the brand on to his own children. The physical product and the plant used to make it may all have changed beyond recognition, but brand equity, if well managed, can easily outlast these tangible assets.[34]

The relationship between the brand name and brand equity can be subtle. When The Mobile Channel changed its name to Research Now, the aim was to communicate a radical change in the business. In contrast, when OpenVenue merged with RN and switched to using the global RN brand name, the message was almost the opposite: '*Research Now is the new name for the business. We can now offer you a global service but, apart from that additional benefit, the brand promise and our standards of quality, speed, and customer service are unchanged*'. In other cases, such as when Mars's Marathon chocolate bars became Snickers in several countries and when Andersen Consulting became Accenture globally, the core message was that *nothing* had changed except the name.

None of these subtleties change the key issue that the starting point for organic growth is a clear definition of the target market and a customer-relevant brand promise. Building on that foundation, in most markets the main driver of long-term growth is customer-focused innovation, as we discuss more fully in the following chapters. Again, the brand is a key element because of the two-way relationship between brand and innovation:

- Successful innovation reinforces brand equity and for some brands - such as Apple, Gillette, and Zara - lies at its heart
- A strong brand makes customers more willing to try the company's new products and services, and a bit more forgiving if these don't immediately deliver as promised.

### *A natural experiment: the two Germanys*

The relationship between brand and innovation is illustrated by what happened in post-war Germany. When Stalin created the Iron Curtain in 1945, there was no material difference in the level of economic development in East versus West Germany. When the Berlin Wall fell in 1989, West Germany had enjoyed almost continuous increases in productivity and living standards over four decades, driven by exactly the processes described in this book, especially among its many world-class private manufacturing companies (the 'Mittelstand'[35]): a clear, relevant customer promise reliably delivered and relentlessly improved through aggressive, customer-focused innovation, leading to ever-growing brand awareness, relevance and trust within a clearly defined target market. But in East Germany, most of the product and process technologies when the Wall fell had barely changed since the 1940s: if a Hollywood movie director in 1990 wanted a World War 2 Siemens telephone exchange as a prop, there were plenty available and still in use.

Managers in East Germany had little interest, incentive, or even opportunity to pursue the ART of brand-building: why would you care about meeting customer needs better and better - and better than the competition - or in building customer trust or brand equity if (1) this wasn't what you'd been asked to do, (2) information about customer preferences and satisfaction didn't reach you, and (3) there was no effective competition. In contrast, many West German enterprises, following the principles of our organic growth framework, developed strong and valuable brands.

Tellingly, the main exception to the pattern of non-brands and non-innovation under central planning was the few Soviet bloc industries which did face competition, especially those making military hardware for the Warsaw Pact countries and for export. The iconic Soviet brand is the Kalashnikov AK47 assault rifle, which has a clear, relevant brand promise on which it appears to deliver extremely well.

### *Helping the business survive shocks and missteps*

Brands can also help businesses survive shocks and missteps. Consider Toyota's 'sudden acceleration' product recall in early 2010. This caught the company by surprise but it was soon using social media quite deftly as part of its crisis management. It set up a team to monitor and respond with facts to rumors on Facebook and elsewhere, and created a Twitter presence for COO Jim Lentz. The team identified online fans and promoters and sought their permission to distribute their statements on Toyota channels. By drawing on its brand reputation – the reservoir of goodwill earned over decades of delivering on its promise of quality, reliability and durability – it used these new media effectively to neutralize much of the hostility. By March, when the recall was in full swing, Toyota sales were rebounding, with Camry and Corolla topping the rankings of passenger car sales. Brand equity may be intangible, but its value is obvious at times like this. The practical question, then, is how to develop it, as we now discuss.

## The ART of Brand Building

Every brand is unique but every *valuable* brand has three things in common:

- **Awareness** within the target market: if customers are not aware of your brand, you have no brand equity. Brand awareness within the target market is therefore a prerequisite for long-term organic growth.[36]
- **Relevance**: the brand promise must meet a real and significant need within the target market.
- **Trust** (again, within the target market): the brand must reliably deliver on its promise.

We now discuss how to achieve the first two of these, Awareness and Relevance. (Trust, and how to achieve it, is so important that it forms the main topic of the following chapter).

## How to Build Awareness

Awareness is easier to achieve and maintain - at a price - than relevance and trust. If you spend enough money on brand communications (advertising, PR, etc), you can pretty much guarantee to make, and then keep, people in the target market aware of your brand. The challenge is to do this efficiently and effectively. Most significant brands which have been on the market for more than a few years have high enough brand awareness to form a platform for further growth, simply from the cumulative effect of their market presence and communications. However, the task is becoming harder, because customers - especially those with money - are suffering from increasing time pressure and information overload, and also because of the increasing range and complexity of media and methods. That said, awareness can always be achieved at a price.[37]

### *Building awareness for a start-up business*

More challenging is building brand awareness for a start-up business since, almost invariably, it has far fewer resources than an established business to invest in awareness-building communications.

For a B2B start-up like The Mobile Channel, the task wasn't too bad since there was plenty of interest in mobile as a new advertising medium and a relatively small number of companies - media agencies and large advertisers - accounted for much of the potential market. By the time Chris Havemann and Andrew Cooper then redefined the business as Research Now, they already had a base awareness on which to build, although the switch of core target market to mid-sized market research firms meant that there was plenty still to do. In Chris's words,

> 'Our first motivation has always been survival, so the top priority is always to satisfy our existing clients. The way we've grown our client base has been simple, mostly

> through direct sales, trade shows, and word of mouth, including within the larger research agencies'.

With business-to-consumer (B2C) start-ups, the challenge is greater: typically, they have no brand, no customers, no track record, very little money, and only limited time before that money runs out. The RN client acquisition approach - direct selling leading to satisfied customers who then repeat-buy and recommend you to others - is rarely fast enough for a B2C start-up because, usually, the market is too fragmented and the value of each sale is too low. Therefore, most successful B2C start-ups use a combination of two approaches: working with large business partners, and 'buzz'.

### *Working with large business partners*

A large business partner can bring abundant physical, financial, and management resources to a start-up. For instance, the UK online supermarket Ocado was launched as a joint venture with Waitrose, the leading premium supermarket chain. Waitrose supplies the products Ocado sells and delivers and provided 40% of the start-up investment capital in 2001. Conversely, for a consumer products start-up, a partnership deal with a major retailer can provide immediate national exposure and physical distribution. A classic example is Honda when it first came to the US. It was, effectively, a small start-up because of tight Japanese government restrictions on the amount of foreign exchange available to the team sent to the US. The breakthrough was an order from Sears for Honda 50s, which immediately gave it revenue, exposure, and credibility in the huge and daunting US market.[38]

For pure awareness-building, the ideal partner for a B2C start-up may be a media organization. For instance, in January 2008, Globrix was a new UK real estate search engine business. The market was already crowded, but Globrix's technology enabled it to trawl estate agents' websites or accept data input by the agents themselves and therefore generate business for them at no charge.

Its model was relatively low-cost, since it directed home-seekers to the agents' sites rather than hosting the details on its own system. Because Globrix (unlike most competitors) was charging the agents no fee for listing their properties, signing them up was relatively straightforward. But, like all market makers, it needed to attract buyers as well as sellers: its revenue model used a combination of display advertising and various analytical consulting services for the agents, both of which required high reach and traffic among home-seekers. It was therefore launched as a 50-50 joint venture with Rupert Murdoch's News International, publisher of four of the largest national newspapers in Britain, *The Sun, The Times, The News of the World,* and *The Sunday Times*. News International traded free media space for equity in Globrix.[39]

Similarly, the UK research agency and consultancy YouGov has successfully built up significant brand awareness though the public opinion polls it conducts on behalf of national media. Polling represents only a small part of its business, but the resulting media exposure has been the main driver of YouGov's high brand awareness. Like e-Rewards but not Research Now, YouGov also benefits from using the same brand name with both clients and respondents.

Working with a large business partner means that the other company gives the brand both credibility and mass exposure and enables a B2C start-up to build awareness quickly, but of course this comes at a price, such as an equity stake or a hefty commission on sales. Because the larger partner has most of the bargaining power, the relationship and the distribution of the rewards tend to be unequal.

The other option (and they're not mutually exclusive) is to generate free publicity, often referred to as 'buzz'.

### *'Buzz'*[40]

There are two types of buzz, often working in combination: free media coverage and word-of-mouth recommendations (WOM). In the context of start-ups, they both exploit the fact that the company and its product or service are new and therefore, potentially, news. Unfortunately, few new products are so much better or so different from what is already on the market that journalists will enthusiastically write about them and early customers tell their friends about them. (Persuading entrepreneurs to accept this can be a problem). Therefore, the best story for building brand awareness may well be about something else such as a funny or newsworthy publicity stunt or a human interest story about the founder. On the plus side, the media are constantly short of new stories, so if you give them something that will interest their audience, they will run it.

The biggest new opportunity is to create buzz through online social media. Because new stories - of variable validity - can spread online rather like viruses, the deliberate creation of online customer-to-customer communications about a brand is generally referred to as viral marketing. High-impact advertising such as Apple's Mac launch in 1984 has always created word of mouth, which has always been valued by marketers. However, the dramatic rise of online social networking has made viral WOM a critical objective of new product and service launches.

Internet services, unsurprisingly, have been early exemplars, for example, Hotmail, Amazon, eBay, Google, MySpace and Facebook. Non-US examples include the BBC and Guardian online news sites. All of these have been able to create substantial brand awareness with neither a large business partner nor a huge marketing budget. As traditional print advertising continues to fall from favor, we see more well-established players leveraging buzz for success. Apple is a master of buzz, as most recently illustrated with the iPad. Following a hint that the company had a major new product to unveil, Apple offered no details and would not confirm or deny rumors. Fans and industry observers around the world buzzed, speculated and hyped the iPad well ahead of its unveiling by Steve Jobs.[41]

Although most companies don't have the maniacal fervor of Apple fans to exploit, they can still seed buzz among current and target customers. Unilever launched its spray bottle extension of market-leading spread brand *I can't believe it's not butter*, exclusively with a web-based campaign aimed at creating buzz among women aged 35-plus.[42] Similarly, Chad Vogelsong, Marketing General Manager at JVC Mobile, commenting on the successful launch of its in-dash A/V receiver targeted at 18–35 year old men, remarked, 'The most effective way to reach our core customer. … is (to be on) the Web'.[43]

As for viral advertising, our favorite example is Blendtec's inspired *'Will it blend?'* YouTube clips in which its founder demonstrates the blender's power and robustness by pulverising everything from a golf ball to an iPad. Since the campaign launched four years ago, the videos have been viewed more than 100 million times, and sales have increased 700%. Such campaigns must be authentic and true to the brand values and promise. Sony stumbled badly when it paid an agency to create a fake-authentic blog and YouTube video hyping the latest gaming PSP for Christmas 2006. Faced with a storm of online criticism when word of the deceit leaked out, Sony was forced to own up, withdraw the video, and post a contrite apology on the blog. The debacle surely didn't help sales; 2006 holiday shipments were down 75% on 2005.

## How to Build Relevance

After awareness within the target market, the second prerequisite of a valuable brand – and, therefore, of sustainable organic growth – is that the brand promise must be *relevant to that market*. Unlike brand awareness, however, relevance – the R in the ART of brand-building – is not something you can virtually guarantee if you invest the required resources.

A successful brand requires all three of the A, R, and T. During its brief and difficult life, The Mobile Channel successfully built both awareness and trust among blue-chip corporate clients, but what it promised was insufficiently relevant to their mainstream marketing needs to create a viable business: it met only a limited, niche need, as a medium for 'marketing R&D' rather than 'real marketing'. It had the A and the T of the ART but not the R. As Research Now, however, the company developed an extremely relevant offer, adding the missing piece. Because The Mobile Channel had already built significant awareness and trust, Research Now's sales took off much faster than if it had been starting from scratch: potential clients already knew and trusted the people behind it, especially the co-founders Chris and Andrew.

The importance of ensuring that the brand promise is relevant should be obvious, but how to achieve this, and especially how to ensure that the offer remains relevant in a changing market, is far from obvious. There are several serious challenges:

- The fundamental one is simply that it's often hard to know which benefits customers will value most. Sometimes, the customers themselves don't know this, especially in the context of innovations 'beyond the familiar' (discussed in Chapter 5).
- Not everything customers want can be profitably offered at a price they are willing to pay.
- Customers' preferences and priorities (and their willingness and ability to pay) can also vary widely, both between different customers or segments and over time or even in different contexts for the same customer.
- Finally, even if someone in the organization has a good enough understanding of what's most relevant to most customers, this insight achieves nothing unless and until it's communicated to those with the power to act on it and they do so.

How to ensure customer relevance is a running theme of this book. In the following chapters, we discuss the practicalities in the context of reliably delivering the promise, ensuring that product and service improvements and innovations remain customer-relevant, and opening up the organization so that customers' needs and preferences are always taken into account in decision-making.

Before addressing these unavoidable challenges, however, we briefly discuss an avoidable error made by many companies: an overemphasis on differentiating the brand promise from the competition through 'unique selling propositions' (USPs).

### *Marketers' obsession with being different from the competition*

When we published *Simply Better* in 2004, the *Financial Times* gave us a nice review which began,

> 'This is a book about marketing for people who have read too many books about marketing'.[44]

This astute comment refers to the fact that most marketing books place great emphasis on the need to differentiate your brand from the competition by offering something *unique*, not recognizing that this is not necessarily the same as offering something *relevant to customers* – the fundamental principle of marketing. In fact, an overemphasis on being different from the competition will almost always lead to features and benefits that are irrelevant to most customers.

The subtitle of *Simply Better* was *Winning and Keeping Customers by Delivering What Matters Most*. The central argument was that 'what matters most' is rarely a USP. The myth is that customers will buy your product or service only if it offers them something unique (or cheaper), but in reality,

> 'Customers rarely buy a product or service because it offers something unique. Usually, they buy the brand that they expect to meet their basic needs from the category

> – gasoline or strategy consulting or mortgages – a bit better or more conveniently than the competition. What customers want is simply better – not more differentiated – products and services'.[45]

Having written a whole book on this, we won't repeat it all here. We would, however, like to emphasize two points from the earlier book.

First, we're absolutely not against differentiation, but it has to be the *right kind of differentiation*, based on what matters to customers. The evidence is that this is, first and foremost, about reliably delivering the basics at a reasonable price. Perceived differentiation derived from customers' awareness of the brand, the perceived relevance to them of its promise, and their trust that the company will reliably deliver that promise (ART) are, as we've discussed, the foundation of brand equity and long-term organic profit growth. Differentiation for the sake of being different is not. A useful unique feature or benefit which the competition can't initially match is nice to have, and is often the aim of incremental innovation and publicity, but it is no substitute for promising and delivering the basics at a fair price, and the advantage it provides is usually only short-term. In contrast, a strong, trusted, well-managed brand can have an indefinite life.

Secondly, in line with our clear distinction between brand (in the sense of brand equity) and branding (name, logo, advertising, etc), we note that, although the *brand promise* doesn't need to be strongly differentiated, *branding and brand communications* do need to stand out from the crowd in order to be noticed. It's not a coincidence that the person who first proposed the USP, and his best-known disciples, have all been advertising men: in advertising, being different really does have value in itself.[46]

Given this, we cannot underline enough the critical role of building trust – the T in ART. Trust comes from keeping your promises – not from saying 'trust me' – as we discuss in the next chapter.

**Idea check**

***1. Do you know what your customer promise is?***

Have you checked? At your next management team meeting, ask each participant to write down your customer promise. How much difference do you see? Is there a shared interpretation? Are the results even capable of a common interpretation? You need to sort this out. You need one core promise per brand, fully understood and agreed within the top team. If the top team can't answer the question, you aren't yet on Square One.

***2. Do your customers know your promise to them?***

Have you checked? Ask some. You'll most likely find that it is not aligned with your internal view. Find out why. Are they relying on your communications, your salespeople? Perhaps they are relying on friends' or colleagues' recommendations. Whichever, concretely what have they heard? Reconcile this with the results of Question 1 above.

***3. Does everyone in your company know and understand the brand promise?***

Remember the killer question: ask it, for real.

***4. Is your brand promise really relevant to customers? Have they moved on?***

Again, have you checked? How well, and how recently?

CHAPTER THREE

# DELIVERING TODAY'S PROMISE BETTER AND BETTER EVERY DAY

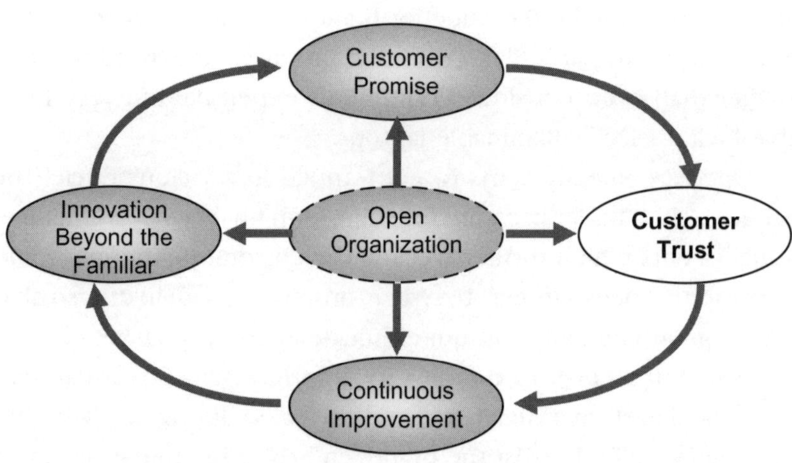


*'Oh wad some power the giftie gie us*
*To see oursel's as others see us!'*

- Robert Burns (1759-96), Scotland's Most Celebrated Poet.[47]

In Chapter 2, we saw how having and communicating a strong, relevant customer promise is the first essential for long-term organic profit growth. We now turn to customer trust, the T in the ART of brand-building. Unlike brand awareness, trust can't be bought (e.g. by telling the customer 'trust me'): it has to be earned. The only way to do this is by reliably delivering your brand promise - both the explicit core promise and everything else customers implicitly and reasonably assume that you will provide.

However clear and relevant your brand promise, unless you relentlessly deliver on it you will never build a strong brand and you will never achieve lasting organic profit growth. In extreme cases, brands that consistently fail to deliver on their promises generate growing customer dissatisfaction, defection, and negative word-of-mouth and eventually disappear from the market. The mushrooming of 'Brand X sucks' websites and online social media means that negative word-of-mouth is now on steroids: increasingly, there's nowhere to hide for brands that don't deliver on the basics or their particular customer promise, and retribution is swifter than ever: consider Kryptonite's expensive but very pickable lock, or Dell's flammable laptops.

Once a company starts to get trapped in a vicious circle, the danger is that, under pressure for short-term financial performance, it makes cuts which further weaken the customer experience and increase the negative gap between promise and delivery, so that even a great company can quite quickly become a basket case, as happened in 2008–9 to Circuit City, a former Wall Street darling.

It is therefore crucial for executives to know (a) whether customers really do trust the brand, and (b) what things are most likely to erode that trust. That's why the 'killer question' for this chapter is:

**'Can every member of your top team list the three things that most erode trust among existing customers?'**

*Every* business should have an explicit system to enable it to 'see itself as others see it'. You should not assume that all the 'good' attributes your company designed into its brand are still visible and relevant to customers. Moreover, if you don't already have a formal process for tracking, communicating, and following up the sources of customer dissatisfaction, you are missing out on one of the simplest and lowest-risk ways of increasing your long-term profits. You need to *know* what's most annoying and disappointing your customers, especially your most valuable ones, so that you can fix it before they abandon and bad-mouth you. Get it wrong and you undermine the foundation required for the innovation that will secure sustainable organic growth.

Here we focus on the three main building blocks of this foundation.

- First, we emphasize **the primacy of customer dissatisfaction** with your brand. Satisfaction and dissatisfaction are somewhat different coins. Because customer dissatisfaction typically has a bigger (negative) impact on the brand than the (positive) impact of satisfaction, and because the drivers of dissatisfaction are often easy to elicit from angry or disappointed customers, we recommend that discovering and addressing these drivers should be your first priority. The challenge of doing so is more psychological and political than technical.
- Second, although measuring customer dissatisfaction and satisfaction is an essential starting point for improving the customer experience, it is no more than that. In order to develop an effective response, you need a **range of diagnostic data**, including both formal metrics and direct customer contact, and ideally a formal model of the determinants of customer satisfaction and – especially – dissatisfaction. Above all, you need to be committed to action.
- Finally, improving the customer experience is rarely costless, so you need to **prioritize** and to manage both costs and customer expectations. This raises a number of issues, especially where other parties control large parts of the

customer experience or where a small minority of unreasonable customers consume disproportionate resources and are impossible to satisfy.

As background, we discuss a case study of a company that has a very clear customer promise, and how it used data on customer dissatisfaction to get the entire organization focused on delivering both the core promise and customers' other expectations.

## Aggreko – Absolute Reliability, Absolutely

Washington, DC, January 20, 2009. Barack Obama arrives for his inauguration as 55th US President in the presence of eight Supreme Court justices, 99 senators, over 400 congressmen, around 200 official representatives from other countries, 2 million ordinary citizens, and 10 000 army and security personnel. Hundreds of millions of other people around the world will see the event on television.

Everything has been planned to the last detail. There is no margin for error. All contractors are best in class and deemed totally reliable – not 95%, 99% or even 99.9% reliable, absolutely totally reliable. Providing secure electrical power to the many temporary military command stations, media centers, sound and video relays, and emergency medical stations is Aggreko, headquartered in Glasgow, Scotland – just as it has done for every inauguration since President Clinton's first one in 1993.

With around 3600 employees in over 140 permanent locations in 34 countries offering 24/7 coverage and back-up, Aggreko has become the world leader in the rental of essential power and temperature control by delivering on its brand promise: *exceptional service and total reliability, period*. As well as the US Government, customers include top sporting events (Olympic Games, Soccer World Cup Finals, US PGA Open golf championship, Daytona 500) and emergency relief teams following major natural disasters. More routinely, countries, cities and companies rely on Aggreko to provide power on both a short- and long-term basis. In doing just this, and only this, Aggreko has become a $1.61 bn company generating pre-tax profits of $383m in 2009, growing a further 19% year-on-year in the first half of 2010.

### *Scratching an itch*

When Rupert Soames was appointed CEO of Aggreko in 2003, his background gave a clear sense of how he would lead the company. He had spent his early career working for Lord Weinstock, one of Britain's best-known industrialists. Weinstock, head of the General Electric Company (GEC), was well known for running his business by its financial and operational numbers. Soames was the same: tough, data-driven, analytically strong, and ambitious. CFO Angus Cockburn remembers his initial meeting with Soames. It was scheduled to last two hours but continued well beyond that into the evening through dinner. *'The man obviously knew more about Aggreko than any human being on the planet,'* recalls Cockburn.[48]

What was less obvious at the time was Soames's passion for delivering customer value. At GEC, he had put his home phone number on the company's dishwasher brochures. This led to a painful induction to the world of customer dissatisfaction. One morning, at 4 o'clock, the phone rang and the caller told him, *'Mr Soames, your dishwasher broke down at the end of a party for 250 people. I have just finished washing everything up by hand. Good night'.*[49] Soames's customer mantra thereafter was: get it right first time. This enthusiasm for 'doing right by the customer' was responsible for what he calls his 'itch':

> 'Like it or not, even the wisest manager, who fully buys into the merit of building long-term value, is in truth operationally preoccupied and motivated by the here and now – today, this month, this quarter and this year. While I like this in many ways, I have long been concerned that this very natural mentality places marketing and customer

> support spend in the firing line all the time. Cutting back on these looks like a quick short-term win when you're in a squeeze, but can clearly be a longer-term disaster. Management systems haven't provided managers the complete picture they need to run their businesses for the short *and* long term. The accumulation or otherwise of customer equity has not been transparent.'

What he really wanted – the 'itch' he wanted to scratch – was an enhancement of the management systems he'd learned under Weinstock and brought to Aggreko. He wanted data that would give a clear, regular and reliable indicator of how the company was performing *in the eyes of customers*. So when Simon Lyons, Aggreko's Global Marketing Director, suggested in mid 2006 that the company become a relatively early adopter of the Net Promoter Score (NPS), Soames saw a way to scratch that itch.

### *The Net Promoter Score (NPS)*

> 'NPS is one number, it's easy to interpret, it's easy to collect, the bigger it is the better, it gets noticed, it is transparent and it is actionable.'
>
> – Rupert Soames.

The Net Promoter Score (NPS) is somewhat controversial and widely misunderstood, so it's worth spelling out how it works and what it does and doesn't provide. It was developed by customer loyalty guru Fred Reichheld at management consultancy Bain and launched in 2003 under the slogan, *'The one number you need to grow'*.[50] Reichheld argued that customer recommendations are a potent driver of new business. If the recommendation is to a friend or colleague, it will be especially thoughtful and certainly not offered lightly, implying a higher threshold than 'mere' satisfaction. Willingness to recommend is therefore highly correlated with customer loyalty as well as with new customer acquisition, and negatively correlated with the unit cost of marketing, making it a strong predictor of profitable organic growth.

The specific question Reichheld proposed, and which forms the basis of NPS, is: *'How likely is it that you would recommend company/brand X to a friend or colleague?'*, with a scale from 'Not at all likely' = zero to 'Extremely likely' = 10.

'How Likely Is It That You Would Recommend Company/Brand X to a Friend or Colleague?'

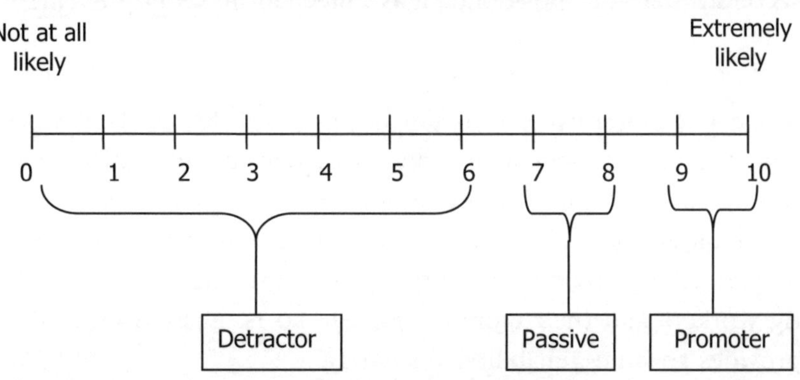


The results are reduced to a single number, the Net Promoter Score, using a simple, very tough, scoring system:

- Only customers scoring 9 or 10 are labeled 'Promoters'.
- Those scoring 7 or 8 are called 'Passives' and ignored in the NPS.
- Those scoring zero to 6 are 'Detractors'.

The Net Promoter Score is simply the % of respondents who are Promoters minus the % who are Detractors:

**NPS = (% Promoters) minus (% Detractors)**

The NPS is not without its critics, as we discuss later, but it was exactly what Rupert Soames was looking for. Convincing him to adopt it wasn't difficult but Aggreko managers were used to running their own fiefdoms and being judged on their financial and operational numbers. What Soames and Lyons were now proposing was that, *in addition to* these metrics, the NPS numbers too would flow through the organization. If the customer feedback was lower in a particular geographical area, the boss would immediately know and so would the boss's boss, right up to the CEO.

What led to the acceptance of NPS was, first, that the top management team, especially the CEO, were fully committed to it and, secondly, that they positioned it as a mechanism for improvement.

### *A shock on the Gulf Coast*

Bruce Pool, Aggreko's General Manager for the US Gulf Coast region, is a confident man - and with reason. He and his team supply power to the offshore drilling and extraction operations of major oil and gas companies such as Chevron. Their generators power drill equipment, living quarters and rig electronics. To the rig workers and their employers, Aggreko is 'mission critical'. It provides absolute reliability, absolutely.

Over the years the company enjoyed success due to its superior resources and scale (kit, manpower, engineering capabilities, and infrastructure) relative to its mostly local competitors. When Bruce Pool learned of Soames's 'big idea' he was delighted. He felt that his team had really nailed their customer commitments and built a reputation as a 'can do' crew: no challenge was too daunting, no problem too complex, no timeline too short. They were good, and were proud of being good. NPS would prove it!

When the first NPS results arrived, Pool was shocked to find them less positive than he had expected. Overall the data painted a positive picture. As expected, most customers were 'promoters'. What stunned him, however, was that a significant minority were 'detractors'. It was a huge blow to learn that quite a few customers - people he thought he knew well and who he felt liked him and were positive about the company - would not only not recommend others to buy from Aggreko, but would quite likely specifically advise them not to do so. It just didn't make sense.

### *Following up with the detractors*

Determined to get to the bottom of things, Pool pulled together a small team to dig into the data, talk to the detractors, and find out what was bugging them. When they regrouped a few days later, the picture became clear - surprising but clear. Everyone, including the detractors, agreed that Aggreko was very good at delivering on its core promise of reliable power supply. The problem was that these customers were dissatisfied with other aspects of the service experience that Pool could easily imagine, but hadn't realized were important. For instance, detractors complained that:

- The salespeople weren't as savvy as expected. Pool had known that there was variance in the team but had assumed that this didn't get in the way of getting the job done.
- Aggreko's invoices were complex and hard to tie back to the original quotations. Again, Pool had known this and simply accepted it: Aggreko's service is complex so its billing was complex too.

Some detractors ridiculed an earlier effort to introduce a significant equipment upgrade. As Pool puts it, *'We added some really cool features'*: generator rigs were adapted with sophisticated programming to give customers added flexibility and the option of remote monitoring and analysis. Yet, with all these new bells and whistles, clients couldn't rent the equipment. The detractors helped Pool see that these 'enhancements' were, to most of them, just unwanted complications.

One detractor complained bitterly about late delivery, yet Aggreko's operating standards had been met and the transaction record showed delivery as being 'on-time'. It transpired that there had been a complete misunderstanding between Aggreko and the customer about what had been promised. Expectations had been misinterpreted. Further analysis showed that such misunderstandings were not uncommon.

### *Addressing the issues*

Pool and his team were jolted into a new reality. They were less well in touch with customers than they had believed. Three quick and simple, but costly, decisions were taken:

- Training for sales people was adapted to get the whole team with no exceptions up to 'top-gun' standard.
- A program was instituted to solve the invoicing issue - the mantra: simplify, simplify, simplify.
- Finally, more rigorous and explicit service agreements were introduced to minimize misunderstandings with customers.

Needless to say, the NPS numbers for this region soon started improving. The challenge now is to keep the NPS scores improving by reducing these and other irritants while still ensuring delivery of the core brand promise (absolutely reliable power supply) and meeting the other tough financial and operating targets.

### *NPS at Aggreko today*

The NPS of Aggreko's North American operation now ranks ahead of well-known customer service champions such as Amex, Southwest Airlines, Ebay and Fedex, and is roughly on a par with the likes of Harley-Davidson, Costco, USAA and Amazon. Soames is delighted but believes that there is still substantial scope for improvement.

Today, NPS is fully embedded in the management control system. Every week Aggreko's 'Power Pack', its management information package, goes to all directors and business leaders and their teams. Along with the critical data you'd find in most management control systems (sales, order book, headcount, receivables, fixed asset utilization and so on) NPS is prominently displayed. Managers know that negative variances will give rise to questions that can be answered only if they've gone to the source of the apparent problem, explored the issues thoroughly, and addressed them.

NPS scores for each region also form part of the information sent to the executive committee every month, enabling the top team to check whether Aggreko is delivering on its brand promise - the total customer experience as well as the core brand benefit of absolutely reliable power supply - better and better every day. The whole cycle of reporting and follow-up is a process of customer-relevant continuous improvement.

## The Primacy of Customer Dissatisfaction

The Aggreko case highlights one of the points made at the start of this chapter: the power of customer dissatisfaction to undermine brands, often because the company has failed to provide something basic which the customer took for granted. Usually, this is something which was once an innovation and a source of positive satisfaction, but which customers now simply assume as part of the standard product or service.

Consider automatic teller machines (ATMs). Definitions vary, but what we know today as ATMs were first introduced in 1969 by Chemical Bank in New York, to much fanfare.[51] Today, ATMs are a commodity. They no longer distinguish one bank from another and are not a significant source of positive customer satisfaction - yet they can certainly cause dissatisfaction. Imagine you are on a business trip to an unfamiliar city and find that the only ATM near your hotel is out of order, out of cash, or has a problem with your specific card. At that moment, how do you feel about that bank? Grateful to it for providing a conveniently located ATM - thanks for trying? Absolutely not: you feel enraged and let down.

Contrast this with the same situation where the ATM works - as in, you get the cash. How does that feel? Has your attitude to the bank changed as a result of the transaction? Not at all. The chances are, minutes after getting the cash you'll have forgotten it.

Think about the impact on the brand. An ATM that works will do little if anything to increase customer satisfaction and strengthen brand equity apart from reinforcing awareness. But one that doesn't work will create dissatisfaction and may perceptibly damage the brand.

### *Stop annoying and disappointing your customers*

It's in the nature of competitive markets that innovations such as ATMs get copied and, over time, become part of the basics. Safety and reliability features of cars like airbags and ABS are another example. The mistake is then to assume that they no longer matter. True, they have limited potential to *increase* brand equity, but they have significant potential to *reduce* it. And, despite the fact that every CEO knows the importance of customer focus, firms still routinely let their customers down, leading to widespread customer dissatisfaction and large, persistent variations between competitors on standardized satisfaction scores such as NPS and the American Customer Satisfaction Index (ACSI).

For instance, a study by management consultants McKinsey and the Better Business Bureau in 2004 found that the worst-performing US mobile operator received *5.7 times* as many complaints per million subscribers as the best operator.[52] These are not 10, 20, or 30 percent differences, they are huge differences. And if customers take the trouble to complain, in most cases they are really annoyed and likely to tell other people.

Sometimes, customers' annoyance drives them to extremes. In 2005, Ashley Gibbons (26) had been put on hold for an hour while trying to order a broadband internet connection from UK cable company NTL. While randomly pressing keys on his phone, he stumbled across the facility to change NTL's recorded message – the one that interrupts the soothing music every two minutes to say something like, *'Please wait. Your call is important to us. One of our operators will be with you shortly'*. He left the following message, heard repeatedly by all the other customers kept on hold over the next hour or so:

> 'Hello, you are through to NTL customer services. We don't give a -- about you, basically, and we are not going to handle any of your complaints. Just -- off and leave us alone. Get a life.'[53]

It is a dangerous myth that, in today's competitive markets, the basics - like safe and reliable cars, accurate billing, ATMs that work, and answering the phone promptly - have become mere 'table stakes'. The myth is that all serious competitors have to provide these basics so they are no longer a source of differentiation and competitive advantage.

In reality, because reliably delivering the basics is so difficult, firms continue to vary significantly in their ability to do so and, because customers care so much about these issues, *when the company fails to provide them*, they can indeed be a source of sustainable competitive advantage for the better managed firms. This was a central part of our argument in *Simply Better*.

Similarly, *all* the examples of successful companies in this book are, most of the time, better than their competitors at *not annoying and disappointing their customers*. Of course that isn't their primary mission, but it's a key part of the hidden foundation on which everything else is built.

### *Your first priority*

The implication is clear: your *first priority should be to identify and reduce the drivers of customer dissatisfaction with your brand.* The main drivers usually reflect failure to provide some of the basics, as we've discussed, but can include egregiously bad performance on product or service features (such as fuel economy or, in service businesses, polite staff) which also have the potential to provide positive customer satisfaction. You'll almost certainly need to fix a number of basic things in order to ensure that you're reliably delivering the current brand promise to meet customer expectations, before you switch your main focus towards improving the brand promise (and customer expectations) – the topic of the next chapter.

It's important both to be impatient (like Rupert Soames) and to take the long view (also like Rupert Soames). People sometimes talk as if there were an inherent trade-off between improving your delivery of the basics and innovating to get ahead of the competition. In the short term, that's true, to the extent that you have only so much management attention, but in the long run it's wrong: reliably delivering on your current promise builds the trust that lies at the heart of every successful brand (the T in ART) as well as a culture based on customer focus, openness, high standards, and attention to detail. These, in turn, provide the basis for successful customer-focused innovation – the primary driver of lasting organic profit growth, which is what this book is about.

### *Why do companies find this difficult?*

Intellectually, there is nothing hard about any of this. Surely, it's plain common sense that, before you start doing difficult and risky things like innovation, you should first do the easier things which are almost guaranteed to increase long-term profits, such as not annoying your customers. But the fact that companies routinely let their customers down on the basics suggests that putting these ideas into practice is not at all easy. Why?

Some of the issues are psychological and political. One underlying problem is that taking the customer's perspective rather than one's own – including what Robert Burns called the 'giftie' of seeing ourselves as others see us – goes somewhat against human nature. Our own and our colleagues' lives and problems inevitably capture more of our attention than those of our clients and customers. As an adman told one of us in an unguarded moment, 'You do know everyone hates the client, don't you?' – an exaggeration, but not a complete fiction.

We have no recommendations for changing human nature but there is an important practical implication here, because the extent to which people are interested in helping other people varies significantly between individuals, depending on their genes, early upbringing, and so on. The recommendation is to recruit people with the right values, even if others have more relevant experience and knowledge.

For instance, First Direct, the UK's first telephone bank, launched with a brand promise based on superior customer experience. For its call center - the primary customer touch point - it therefore primarily recruited 'people people' such as teachers and nurses, rather than people with previous experience of UK retail banking. To make this work, it needed to train its recruits in the necessary knowledge and skills, support them with outstanding IT systems in order to limit how much they needed to know, and have excellent first-level supervisors.

Obviously, this is a question of balance - law firms need lawyers that are technically first class as well as lawyers with good client skills (and, ideally, some strong on both dimensions) - but the general idea that it's easier to teach people new knowledge and skills than to change their basic values and personality still applies. Other psychological and political reasons why companies keep letting down their customers are that:

- It's more inspiring to work on things that are new, exciting and, potentially, even newsworthy than on minor improvements in order to annoy customers less. We discussed the seductive glamour of heroic, headline-grabbing radical innovation in Chapter 1.
- By definition, whenever customers are dissatisfied, either someone or some system is at fault, or could at least have performed better. In addition, dealing with dissatisfied customers is rarely fun - recall the middle-of-the-night phone call to Rupert Soames about the broken dishwasher.

We return to these challenges in later chapters. In the rest of this one, we now discuss two other difficult execution issues:

- First, in order to address the drivers of customer dissatisfaction, you need a *range of different types of data.*
- Secondly, you also need to manage *costs and customer expectations.*

In combination with the psychological and political challenges, these are the factors that make it hard for companies to get the basics right - and which, therefore, provide a sustainable competitive advantage to the few companies that address them successfully.

## You Need a Range of Data

In Aggreko, Rupert Soames found that the Net Promoter Score (NPS) gave him exactly what he needed to bring customer satisfaction and, especially, dissatisfaction into his numbers-based management system. But of course the NPS numbers themselves don't do anything to improve the customer experience.

What NPS and similar metrics do in the context of a business like Aggreko is to highlight which regions and units have an above-normal proportion of detractors in each reporting period. The improvement process then works mainly because the managers of those regions and units work their butts off to find out why some of their customers are unhappy, and then do whatever they can to reduce or remove the source of the problem. The local managers also talk to their bosses to discuss the data, the problems, and the solutions, especially if the problem is company-wide, as with the invoicing system. But in this particular company, most issues can be addressed locally because:

- Local management is close to its customers (enabling it to uncover the sources of dissatisfaction quickly with no help from head office) and has most of the resources to be able to respond, and

- The tough, numbers-driven corporate culture ensures that they do so promptly.

This is unusual. In most companies, management at all levels needs a wider range of formal data to flag up problems, diagnose their causes, and support follow-up. The role of NPS and other simple measures of customer satisfaction/dissatisfaction is the same as at Aggreko – to provide a flashing light, drawing attention to a problem and highlighting where it is within the business. That's it: NPS and other simple, generic customer satisfaction/dissatisfaction metrics stop at this point. The next stage is to collect and analyze more diagnostic data to uncover what is causing the problem, and then to look at how it can be fixed. It is at this follow-up stage that one needs more detailed and context-specific data, analysis, and planning.

This distinction between simple, universal satisfaction metrics such as NPS and more complex, context-specific diagnostics sounds obvious but is widely misunderstood. Most market researchers hate NPS. This partly reflects the way Fred Reichheld positioned it when he launched it, but also says something about what's wrong with many market researchers.

### *Why market researchers hate NPS and why they're wrong*

Market researchers hate NPS because they say it wastes information, lacks diagnostic value, and fails to perform as advertised:

- It wastes information because it treats all 'detractors' (scoring anything from zero to 6) identically, and similarly for the 'passives' (scoring 7 or 8) and the 'promoters' (scoring 9 or 10). In contrast, a traditional average would use all the information.

- It reduces everything to a single number which tells us nothing about what is *driving* customer satisfaction/ dissatisfaction.
- It does not, as sometimes claimed, predict organic growth better than traditional measures of customer satisfaction.[54]

All these criticisms are correct but, in our view, miss the point. NPS and other simple measures of customer satisfaction/dissatisfaction are a 'cattle prod' to jolt the organization - or a particular unit within it - into action. Recall how the results for Aggreko's Gold Coast region came as a shock to the regional manager Bruce Pool. NPS is well designed for this purpose because:

- It's a single number which provides a common language that everyone can understand
- Its potential range is from −100 to +100: the actual numbers vary widely, unlike a typical 5-point satisfaction scale where in practice most scores fall within a range from about 3.0 to 4.5, which sounds much less
- It uses emotive terms like 'promoter' and 'detractor' which further help to capture people's imagination.

In order to drive change, you need to engage people emotionally as well as rationally. NPS is well suited to achieving this. That's why leading companies such as GE, Microsoft, Intuit, Allianz, Enterprise, Target, and Dell have embraced it enthusiastically. The same effect can be achieved using any satisfaction/dissatisfaction scale to produce NPS type scores, but you need to adopt a similarly hard line on what constitutes a promoter or detractor. For instance, with a typical 1-to-5 scale, you could use (% saying 5) minus (% saying 1, 2, or 3). People will almost certainly try to persuade you to soften this, e.g. by including the 4s as promoters and/or treating the 3s as passives. Just say no.

### *Other data: why market researchers are also right*

Where market researchers are right is in emphasizing the need to supplement the initial satisfaction score 'cattle prod', wherever it comes from - NPS, ACSI, Gallup or other sources. Managers need guidance after they've gotten over the prod. At this point, they need richer data, both quantitative and qualitative, that explain *why* customers are dissatisfied.

Many of the relevant measures are likely to be highly context-specific, perhaps requiring an ad hoc research project. Others will be more general, while still helping to address the 'why?' question. For instance, for retailers, the standard ACSI metrics include - in addition to the overall satisfaction index - several measures of customer expectations, perceived product and service quality, value for money, complaint handling, and so on.[55]

To supplement formal market research, other sources of relevant insight include *direct customer contact* - face to face, by phone, and online - in which managers and sales and service people talk to individual customers and ask about problems and how the company could deliver better on its brand promise, be easier to do business with, and ensure that the promise stays relevant.

Increasingly, executives are going further than this, spending time on their own company's shop floor or even on the shop floor of a B2B customer, in order to get a fuller understanding of the practical day-to-day issues. Every executive member of the Tesco board still spends a week a year on the shop floor, stacking shelves and serving customers. They don't always enjoy it but it tells them a lot about what's really happening at the sharp end, including the weaknesses of their internal systems. It also sends a strong signal to the whole workforce about the company's commitment to customer focus, the importance of front-line staff, and execution.

Similarly, Kuljit Kaur, head of business development at employee incentives company P&MM, has worked undercover in clients' call centers and car dealerships in order to learn at first hand what it feels like to work there: *'We find that many of our clients don't really understand what motivates people at the sharp end'.*[56]

A related, more formal, data source is *mystery shoppers*, who can tell you in detail what the customer experience is like, if necessary testing specific aspects of the service.

### *Customer complaints and lapsed customers*

Finally, a crucial source of insights on customer dissatisfaction is *complaints*. Everyone knows that customer complaints have the potential to help companies improve their delivery of the brand promise, as well as often suggesting ways to make that promise more relevant, but few organizations use this rich source as actively and systematically as they could. You should positively encourage people to complain if they're disappointed, and then:

- Monitor trends, to see which problems seem to occur most and/or seem to be increasing, in order to prioritize your improvement efforts
- Follow up significant individual cases with a root cause analysis and action plan to reduce the likelihood of a recurrence.

An additional benefit of following up complaints quickly and vigorously is that outstanding service recovery usually repairs the damage to the brand in the mind of the complainant and sometimes even leads to *more* loyalty than before the problem occurred.

A related, even richer, source of well-informed dissatisfaction data is *lapsed or defected customers*. These are people who know your brand well and have chosen to take their business elsewhere. If you can reach them, they can tell you a lot about where you have been going wrong. Again, there is always a chance of bringing them back to your brand if you convince them that you really want their business and will correct whatever drove them away (assuming it wasn't just an insanely low price from a competitor).

Of course, following up customer complaints and lapsed customers raises all the psychological and political challenges we discussed before, even more than the other sources of insight about the drivers of customer dissatisfaction with your brand. Unfortunately, in the words of Jane Fonda, *'No pain, no gain'*.

## Managing Costs and Customer Expectations

The final issue for this chapter is the need to manage costs and customer expectations. Plowing money into ever more product or service enhancements along the same tried and trusted dimensions will not necessarily increase customer satisfaction if expectations continue to rise. One study found that expectations of a third of consumers had risen within the last 12 months while just over a half reported they had higher expectations of goods and services they buy compared with five years earlier.[57]

Expectations do not come from thin air. We form them based on our previous experience of using the product or service, our interpretation of advertisements, personal interactions with sales and other front line staff, independent reviews (now more pervasive and influential than ever before - witness the power of sites such as www.tripadvisor.com) and often spontaneous appraisals and recommendations from friends (also increasingly online).

One problem seems to be 'sloppy' advertising and other promotions along with loose-lipped, over-promising sales staff *('Suits you, Sir', 'We'll have it on Monday'*, even, *'Yes, that flight will depart on time'*). This can be easily fixed by outing culprits and carefully reviewing paid promotions and front line behavior, particularly ensuring that incentives are not wittingly or unwittingly encouraging misrepresentation. More problematic are customer blogs that carry innocently motivated but incorrect claims about features and performance, including about rumored future products such as Apple's iPhone and iPad before they launched.

### *Customers sometimes hold you responsible for other people's mistakes*

Frustratingly, customers don't know or really care where one provider's responsibility ends and another's begins. Consider your typical journey by air. There are dozens of opportunities for something to go wrong in ways that materially and negatively impact the quality of your trip. Lack of sufficient ground-side or air-side transportation, misinformation during check-in, long and slow security lines, poor service at an airport restaurant or store, overcrowding or excess noise in an airline lounge, inefficient boarding, delayed baggage retrieval or worse, expensive taxis on arrival, a hotel not quite ready to provide you a room although you requested early check-in, the list is endless.

For most journeys, not one of these procedures is under the direct control of the airline, but they frame your in-flight experience and color your recollection of it. If everything goes well, the airline will benefit from your positive total customer experience and satisfaction. Hence the investments by many airlines to extend customer care for their most valuable customers beyond the actual flight, and increasingly from the time they leave their own homes. In addition to the obvious luxuries awaiting first and business class passengers on board, their experience of lounges, security, and ground transport is usually very different from that of the typical passenger.

For high-value customers this makes sense. It may also make sense, however, for airlines to rethink the economics of their model as many business passengers are appalled by their travel experiences, especially after security procedures became so intrusive after 9/11. The credit crunch put a halt (at least, temporarily) to the rapid increase in executive jets, but airlines are starting to lose out to executives lobbying their companies to adopt advanced teleconferencing infrastructure as a way of avoiding flying.

The general advice is to understand – and, as far as possible, manage – the end-to-end customer experience rather than just the customer's experience of your brand. Reframe the task so that you take responsibility for this full customer experience through the way you manage the relevant partnerships: ideally, become the dominant partner for the category.

At the same time, you should be explicit about your role, your undertakings within the system and your work on behalf of customers to enhance those parts of the system you do not control. Above all, be explicit both about what you *are* promising and about what you *are not* willing to be held accountable for. This last is a critical part of managing customer expectations: customers need to know what you can deliver, but also, even implicitly, what you cannot.

### *Costs and unreasonable customers*

The inevitable need to manage costs is usually the biggest challenge in reducing the drivers of customer dissatisfaction. In today's competitive and, increasingly, global markets, the pressure to reduce costs is relentless, creating a need for continuous *process* innovation to meet customers' expectations of improved value for money, even when their expectations of product and service features, quality, and reliability are steady or increasing. There are no general answers here, except that, as always, it's crucial to have good customer insights as well as effective and efficient operations, in order to set the right priorities about what to enhance, what to retain, and what to cut back or eliminate in order to reduce costs. Part of the value of good customer insights is to help you stop projects which will have little impact on customer satisfaction.

In addition, some customers are simply impossible to satisfy. Irrespective of how simple, clear and compelling your value proposition is and how well you deliver on both your explicit promises and those implicit standards that customers reasonably expect of all brands in your category, there will always be some customers who are still dissatisfied.

Beyond a certain point, you should stop worrying about them: there is nothing you can do to make them happy. Instead, your task is to ensure that they do not suck up too many resources. Thus, in your customer analysis, you should control for 'the utterly unreasonables', that is, irrational customers who can never be satisfied. Identify them, do your best until you determine you cannot turn them around, and at that point, fire them. That's right; just get them off your books.

When Debra Brede discovered just how time-consuming, distracting and unprofitable a small number of accounts were for her investment management firm, she encouraged them to take their business elsewhere. Getting rid of them enabled her to devote more time to business development. As a result, profits rose 25% the year following the purge compared with about 9.5% in each of the previous few years.[58]

Apparently following the same logic, in June 2007 Sprint Nextel fired 1100 customers whose expectations they decided they were just unable to meet (see Figure 3.1). One report suggested that these 'serial complainers' called customer service 40 to 50 times a month, more than 40 times the norm.[59]

Sprint was subjected to a damaging public outcry. The reason why some companies can successfully 'fire' customers while others encounter difficulties is that those to be fired should be total outliers in a context of a company really intending to achieve total satisfaction. In 2007, Sprint's ACSI score was 61 against an industry average of 68 – itself well below most service industries (which, in turn, tend to be lower than manufacturing industries). Since then, Sprint has gone backwards. In 2008 its ACSI score plummeted to 56 while the industry stood still at 68 and industry leader Verizon inched ahead from 71 to 72.[60] For years, Sprint has had a reputation for poor customer service and poor network coverage. It is one of the most unloved companies, with one of the worst churn records, in an industry not known for generating high levels of customer satisfaction and loyalty.[61]

Despite the backlash when it said 'enough is enough' to these 1100 customers, we remain convinced that Sprint did the right

Figure 3.1: Sprint Letter

Date: June 29, 2007

Re: Account:

Dear ,

Our records indicate that over the past year, we have received frequent calls from you regarding your billing or other general account information. While we have worked to resolve your issues and questions to the best of our ability, the number of inquiries you have made to us during this time has led us to determine that we are unable to meet your current wireless needs.

Therefore, after careful consideration, the decision has been made to terminate your wireless service agreement effective July 30, 2007. This will allow you to pursue and engage with another wireless carrier.

We understand that having to switch to another wireless carrier may be an inconvenience, and we want to do everything possible to help you during this transition. So, a credit has been applied to your account to bring your current balance to zero. In addition, we will not require you to pay an Early Termination Fee and you are free to transfer (or "port") your number to another non-Sprint Nextel carrier. You will, however, need to initiate the transfer of your number with the carrier of your choice before July 30, 2007 as the number will no longer be available as of that date.

Should you have any questions regarding the transfer of your number to another wireless carrier or about the final adjustments to your account, please call our customer care department at (877) 527-8405.

Sincerely,

Sprint Nextel Corporation

thing. Clearly, it has a lot more work to do to reduce the drivers of customer dissatisfaction, but losing these customers should have freed up significant resources which will be better deployed improving the quality of service for the reasonable majority. By September 2010 these actions and doubtless others were beginning to have an impact. Sprint Nextel's ACSI score reached 70, still behind industry leaders Verizon and T-Mobile[62].

All businesses should identify their most unreasonable customers and be strict in dealing with them. Introduce codes of conduct, instill norms, and if necessary lay down rules that ensure that all customers within a given segment are given an even hand.

When Costco announced that it would not accept returns of televisions, computers, MP3 players and other electronic items after 90 days, it suffered no consumer outcry or backlash.[63] Although this was an adverse new condition, it was accepted for two reasons:

- Costco's measure was unambiguous, reasonable, and set clear expectations for the future.
- Costco already had a strong positive reputation for customer friendliness. With an ACSI of 81, relative to the industry average of 75, its strong brand, built up through millions of customer experiences over time, meant that consumers gave it the benefit of the doubt[64].

Costco has earned its customers' trust and can thus take leadership in protecting the interests of its majority customers. Against this background, ditching some potentially abusive customers to protect the relationship with most customers is the right course of action. Most customers understand the connection between firms' toughness on the unreasonable minority and their ability to provide value to the reasonable majority.

Whatever steps are necessary, however bold and difficult they seem, you must deliver on your current promise. It is *the* essential platform for your future brand, innovation, and growth. The next step demands that you relentlessly improve your brand promise, the subject of Chapter 4.

**Idea Check**

***1. What is your customer satisfaction target?***
Why? Which perspective are you taking, that of the accountant, the quality director, the general manager or the customer? You need a stretch target which shows everyone in the company that the customer is king.

***2. What is your customer satisfaction score?***
How well is it shared among the key people in your organization - that's everyone who impacts on whether you keep your promise to your customer? That would be everybody.

***3. How widely do you share your customer dissatisfaction report?***
Yes, DISsatisfaction - 'Customer Dissatisfaction Report'. Okay, when you create one, you must get it out there. Mistakes happen. Imperfection abounds. People generally want the opportunity to improve. They really don't set out to upset customers. Give them the information, the tools and the mandate to get working on *'Delivering Today's Promise Better and Better Every Day'*.

***4. How good is your model of the drivers of customer satisfaction and dissatisfaction?***
You have to prioritize. A good model of the drivers will help you concentrate your effort and resources where they will make the most difference to your customers.

# CHAPTER FOUR

# DRIVING THE MARKET BY RELENTLESSLY IMPROVING THE PROMISE

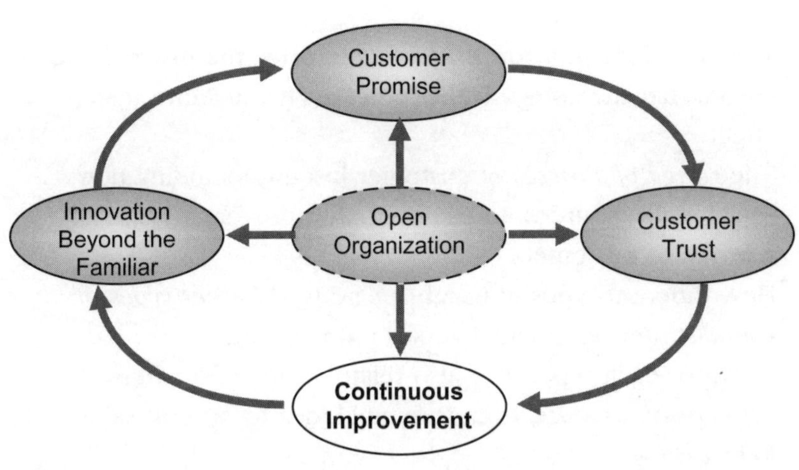


*'There's a way to do better. ... find it'*
- Thomas Edison, Inventor[65]

In competitive markets, brands and their owners cannot sit still. Over time, they have to promise more and more to customers - while still ensuring that they deliver on that improved promise, meeting customers' ever-rising expectations and helping to drive those expectations. This is not a mechanical process: evolving the brand promise involves skill, insight, and judgment. But nor is it just a matter of luck. The best companies get 'lucky' again and again. This chapter is about how they do it through relentless, market-driving incremental innovation, based on ambition to beat the competition combined with good understanding of what customers want. The killer question for this chapter is therefore:

**'Is your brand really the best option for your customers? Will it continue to be next month and next year?'**

The main themes of this chapter are:

- The need for *ambition and focus* to drive the process and ensure that the company's efforts are channeled to maximum effect
- The *range of sources* of customer insight, including new social media sources, to ensure that improvements are all relevant to customers
- How different types of insight relate to *different types of innovation* (incremental versus more radical)
- How, for each type, they also relate to different *stages of the innovation process*, from the initial idea to post-introduction follow-up

The aim is to maintain the flow of creative ideas and ensure that the right ones are acted on. This is about beating the competition not by obsessing about them, nor by trying to be different from them, but by being *more customer-focused, more objectively self-critical, and more constantly dissatisfied with the status quo than your best competitor*. As illustration, we discuss a brand whose long-term success has been based on asking the killer question again and again over six decades.

## Tide: A Textbook Market-Driving Brand

Within consumer packaged goods, the archetypal 'persistent growth' company is Procter & Gamble and the archetypal P&G brand is Tide. For over 60 years, Tide has dominated and driven the US detergent market, perfectly illustrating the approach proposed in this book and achieving a remarkable record of long-term organic profit growth. The Tide brand has, of course, been studied before, from many perspectives. Here, we focus on how its managers have used consumer insights to create continuous, incremental innovation.

The initial launch of Tide in 1946 was a textbook breakthrough technical innovation. The first heavy-duty synthetic laundry detergent, Tide was not just a new product but a new kind of product. It was recognized as a National Historic Chemical Landmark by the American Chemical Society[66] and has been described by P&G's president Neil McElroy as '*The first big change in soap making in 2000 years*'.[67]

Tide's promise was unambiguous. Its launch advertising proclaimed '*Tide Washes Cleanest*'. Cleanest was explicitly defined as 'snowy', 'brilliant', and fragrant. Initially targeted at housewives in areas of hard water, Tide and the other synthetic detergents which followed it soon displaced traditional soaps for laundry washing throughout the USA.[68] Especially in combination with automatic washing machines, it had a big impact on women's lives, saving them many hours of drudgery while producing cleaner laundry.

Even more impressive than its initial success, however, is the way Tide has managed to maintain and even increase its lead over more than six decades. This sustained success is based on P&G's classic, gimmick-free approach, the foundation of which is reliable delivery of a clear, relevant brand promise to both the trade and the consumer - all the issues we've already discussed. We won't repeat that discussion here: you can take it as read that P&G has clear, well-researched brand positioning, tightly manages its product and service quality, quickly follows up customer and consumer complaints, and so on.

Building on that foundation, Tide's long-term success has been created by four other factors:

- Relentless improvement and extension of the brand promise through incremental innovation
- Rigorous use of consumer insights to ensure continuing relevance
- Powerful advertising and other brand support
- Strong leadership and values.

### *Continuous incremental innovation*

Tide has had one of the longest programs of sustained incremental innovation of any product. Even as it was launching, P&G was working on ways to improve both the formula and its production efficiency.[69] According to former chairman A.G. Lafley and consultant Ram Charan, P&G has introduced an average of one Tide-branded product innovation per year ever since launch. The consistent aim of these 60-plus incremental innovations has been to ensure that *'Tide is always the best laundry detergent'*,[70] especially by delivering the core promise – cleaning power – better than the competition. When Colgate and Lever both launched rival products in 1948, *Consumer Reports* confirmed Tide's superior cleaning power.[71] Central to the brand strategy has been a consistent effort to maintain that advantage. Tide has been simply better at delivering the core category benefit.

Importantly, however, Tide's innovations have increasingly gone beyond raw cleaning power. In addition to process innovations to expand capacity and reduce costs, they have included major brand extensions such as Liquid Tide in 1984 and Tide with Bleach in 1988 as well as numerous smaller extensions. For instance, Tide Ultra Concentrate (1992) and Tide 2X Ultra Concentrate (2007) provide benefits to consumers, retailers and the manufacturer by reducing packaging, storage space, and manufacturing and distribution costs.[72]

Commenting on P&G's remarkable success in laundry detergents, John Pepper, former Chairman and CEO, explains the significance of continuous incremental innovation in maintaining Tide's category dominance:

> 'As you develop big-win strategies you must also plan for the small-step improvements that will follow. If you fail to do so, even the most brilliant leaps forward will prove to be unsustainable'.[73]

This view is reinforced by Lafley and Charan who observe that, *'P&G would be a much smaller and much-less-successful company without a steady stream of incremental innovations.'*[74]

In 2001, however, despite its long history of product improvements, Tide was under pressure in the US market. With a 50% price premium in an increasingly competitive market, it faced a weakening value perception.[75] Consumers were saying, 'Yes, Tide is better, but is it *that* much better?'.[76] Many were using cheaper products for everyday purposes while keeping Tide for occasional use with tougher loads of laundry. Household penetration had slowly declined for eight consecutive years: fewer American households were buying Tide - a dangerous trend.[77]

P&G set up a multifunctional team which screened ideas and tested them with consumer research. The result was a series of incremental innovations such as Tide with a Touch of Downy (improved fabric softening), Tide with Febreze (improved deodorizing/freshness), and Tide ColdWater (energy-saving improved cold-water cleaning performance). By 2005, these product improvements had boosted Tide's market share to a commanding 43.2% by value, an increase of 5.8 market share points in just four years.[78] The main source of this renewed growth was P&G's re-emphasis of market-driving incremental innovation.

### *Consumer insights for continuing relevance*

A closely related aspect of the winning formula at P&G has been the company's rigorous use of consumer insights to ensure continuing relevance.

P&G has always been a leader in the use of formal market research to understand how consumers buy and use its products. Like other packaged goods companies, it has long had access to a wide range of quantitative consumer data including:

- usage-and-attitude surveys
- continuous panels measuring household purchases over time
- 'conjoint' studies of consumers' willingness to trade off different product attributes, price, and brand
- 'retail audits' of competing brands' availability in stores
- research on media exposure, advertising awareness, and so on.

All this sophistication, and the emphasis on high-tech analytics and hard, quantitative evidence to support decisions, can have a downside, however. According to Lafley and Charan, in the late 1990s P&G lost its focus on the '*consumer is the boss*' concept.[79] An over-reliance on high-tech techniques may have contributed to a stifling of innovation and prevented P&G's product teams from getting close to consumers. This is a generic issue for packaged goods manufacturers: they have some of the best marketers and data in the world, but no direct contact with consumers. For them, 'customers' are retailers, with whom they have frequent direct contact at many levels.

To counter Lafley's concerns, in the last ten years P&G has greatly increased its use of more 'high-touch' ways of developing consumer insights to supplement - not supplant - 'high-tech' methods. As well as traditional qualitative research techniques, including consumer testing centers and home visits, P&G has started to put more emphasis on newer, more powerful qualitative methods such as online advisory panels of consumers and 'metaphor elicitation' in one-to-one depth interviews, instead of traditional focus groups.

Metaphor elicitation (ZMET) was first developed by Gerald Zaltman at Harvard Business School.[80] It derives from a theory that memory is mainly based on stories and that conscious thoughts often use mental images rather than words. Consumers are asked to bring pictures with them to a semi-structured depth interview. According to Carol Berning, a research fellow in P&G's Fabric & Home Care development team,

> 'These picture techniques work really well. We start people talking about the pictures, and how they reflect their thoughts and feelings about things, and suddenly it's three hours later and the consumer will say: "I didn't think I had that many thoughts and feelings about laundry" or whatever category we're investigating'.[81]

P&G now invests over $200 million per year to understand the 'whole' consumer – who she is, her aspirations, needs, and wants.[82] This has included the development of proprietary research methods to enable deeper understanding across forty product categories in more than eighty countries.[83]

In developing this holistic, 'high-touch' approach, P&G has increasingly moved away from using external qualitative research consultants towards greater use of in-house team members. The philosophy, according to Carol Berning, who trains P&Gers in the required skills, is that, '*You don't hire a moderator and watch them talk to your consumer; you talk to your consumer yourself*'.[84] The advantage is that,

> 'No-one cares about the project as much as you do or knows what you are really looking for, so if you conduct the interview yourself, you have internalized the findings.

It is not like watching a TV program, it's like having a conversation. That's why we do a lot of our own research.'[85]

### *Brand support: how Tide advertising re-engaged with American women*

Despite the success of Tide's product innovations in 2001–05, household penetration continued to decline.[86] The brand team felt that this reflected long-term changes in society. Women still did the family laundry in most US homes but their lives had changed. Most now had full- or part-time jobs. Every year saw a decrease in the number who saw getting the family clothes really clean as fundamental to their identity. Tide's *functional* superiority was becoming less *emotionally* relevant to most consumers. Many also felt that the Tide brand was 'arrogant' and out of touch with their lives.[87] These perceptions had been reinforced by the long-running 'Family Tide' advertising campaign, discontinued in 2000. These ads were set in the laundry room and banged home Tide's functional product performance with a hard-hitting message and tone of voice.

The challenge was to make Tide emotionally relevant to a wider consumer base, including modern women for whom laundry was just part of a busy, fragmented life – and not the most interesting part. P&G knew all about the consumer's shopping and laundry habits, but to reconnect with her, it also needed to understand the rest of her life – its pleasures and pressures, rewards and delights, fears and regrets. It needed a broader understanding of her relationship with fabrics and garments outside the laundry room.

To generate richer insights, a joint team from P&G and Tide's ad agency, Saatchi & Saatchi, was set up to conduct depth research. Traditionally, Tide's market research had focused only on mothers: *'The assumption was that only mothers would do the wash. Yes, they have the greatest number of loads but they are not the only women that we are trying to connect with.'*[88] This time, the subjects would include a wide range of women: working and non-working, single and married, with and without children, and at varying income levels and ages.

The team also wanted to get away from Cincinnati (P&G's home town) and the big metropolitan markets. Instead, they went to Kansas City and Charlotte, Virginia and recruited 25 women whose only common feature was that they all did their own laundry. The team spent a total of three weeks with these women, in their homes, out with their friends, at coffee shops, manicurists, clothes stores, and at dinner. *'If you want to understand how a lion hunts, don't go to the zoo. … go to the jungle'.*[89]

Despite the diversity of these women, there were many commonalities in their lives and in how they defined who they were. For instance:

- ***Full calendars and little time for 'Me':*** *'When I have free time? I barely have time to do my laundry. But when I do, I like to go out with my friends to eat, drink, and socialize'*
- ***Challenge and determination:*** *'What am I most proud of? Being a mom. I'm a great mom! I had to work because my now ex-husband wouldn't do his part'*
- ***Needs for appreciation:*** *'It's nice to be reminded that you are attractive'*
- ***The meaning of garments:*** *'My mom had a stroke last May. I would give her my blanket. I would wash it, make sure it was clean … perfect. I just wanted something of mine that would be close to her while I was gone. It's a blanket I use when I snuggle up to read a book'.*
- ***Women and laundry:*** *'I hate coming home from work, while there are dirty dishes piled up in the sink, laundry to be done'.*

Tide's advertising was missing the mark. It needed to create an emotional link which showed an understanding of real women's lives and what mattered to them. This would represent a radically new approach to advertising P&G's biggest and most iconic brand in its biggest market.

### *The campaign: 'Tide Knows Fabrics Best'*

The new campaign focused on making the brand emotionally relevant to twenty-first century women. One commercial portrayed a working mother's hectic days as a mother, professional, and homemaker. She was first shown in a professional setting wearing white pants and then playing with her daughter in a children's park in the same outfit. The notion is that a working mother doesn't go home and say, *'Oh! Don't bug me, I've got to change first'*. She throws herself on the floor in her work clothes. In another ad, a woman was shown feeding her baby and then being sensuously cuddled by her husband: a mother still wants to be seen as desirable even if she has to make compromises in her other relationships for the sake of her child.

In all the ads, Tide's superior functional performance was included, but clearly connected to the understanding of women's multiple roles. The new slogan *'Tide knows fabrics best'* said nothing about cleaning. *'One of our rallying cries was to get out of the laundry basket and into her life,'* said Kevin Burke, P&G's fabric care marketing director.[90]

The campaign successfully strengthened core users' relationship with the brand while also striking a chord with less committed users. It reversed the long-term decline in household penetration, which increased from 33.6% in 2005 to 37.0% in 2007, while market share increased to an even more commanding 44.5% by value.

The challenge now is to maintain Tide's momentum in a more cost-conscious market and without further increasing the complexity of the product line. That will likely involve some consolidation of sub-brands and variants, while continuing to introduce new and better products under the umbrella brand. In recent years, it has also included strong value messages which explain why Tide is worth the price premium it commands.

### *Strong leadership and values*

Driving and underpinning the extraordinary long-term success of Tide, including its rejuvenation in the last ten years, has been P&G's strong leadership and values. In Chapter 6, we will be discussing organizational culture more fully, so we here simply summarize what we see as the key points at P&G:

- As should be clear from some of the references above, since A.G. Lafley's appointment as CEO in June 2000, P&G has enjoyed strong leadership, focusing on the basics of reliably delivering a clear, relevant, simple promise for each brand, customer and consumer focus, and aggressive innovation, while emphasizing a more 'immersive' approach to consumer research in order to ensure that all innovation is functionally and emotionally relevant.[91]

- Under Lafley, the renewed focus on customers and consumers has been symbolized by reiterating that *'the consumer is the boss'* - a value deeply embedded in P&G's culture, but which had become weaker - and emphasizing simple, powerful ideas such as the *'first moment of truth'* (when the consumer buys the product) and the *'second moment of truth'* (when she uses it).
- As always, P&Gers continue to work hard and with an obsessive attention to detail - another deeply embedded part of the company culture. This obsession is very much in line with the spirit of this book: persistent organic profit growth is mostly about great execution. Attention to detail is a necessary (although, sadly, not sufficient) requirement for this.
- Finally, P&G strives for an open, evidence-based culture: in order to be accepted, proposals need data to support them. This means that the company not only collects extensive consumer data and uses sophisticated techniques to analyze it; it also really uses the results for decision-making and resource allocation.

Having illustrated the argument in the specific context of Tide, we now discuss the four generic issues we introduced at the start of the chapter:

- Ambition and focus
- The range of sources of customer insight
- Insights for incremental versus radical innovation
- The role of customer insights at different stages of the innovation process.

## Ambition and Focus

The need for ambition should be obvious: if you don't aim for market-leading growth, you almost certainly won't achieve it. Apple, Research Now, and Aggreko are all ambitious companies.

Ambition is essential for sustained above-average performance, but offers no guarantees. Motorola fell down on many - perhaps most - of the other issues discussed in this book, so its high ambition was thwarted. Ambition needs to be channeled and focused on a limited number of aims and well-prioritized and executed initiatives to avoid wasting effort and resources.

Less obviously, ambition is not just about setting 'stretch' targets for business performance. It is also about mindset. For instance, the successful companies we feature usually aim to be first with incremental innovations. Their attitude is one of constant dissatisfaction with the way things are, continuous probing and questioning in the search for ways to improve both the delivery of the current promise and the promise itself. They really, really hate to lose market share. Trying to beat their rivals by meeting customers' needs better than the competition acts as an *emotional* driver of better performance.

Focus is partly about the brand promise. The consistent central focus of Tide has always been to get clothes cleaner - the main generic category benefit for detergents, which all brands promise but Tide has consistently delivered 'simply better' than the rest. Similarly, Research Now's core focus has been on 'high-quality online data, on time and on budget', and Aggreko's has been on supplying rented power and other systems with absolute reliability.

This does not mean focusing *only* on the primary brand promise. First, as illustrated by Aggreko, it's essential to deliver the assumed basics - the product and service attributes that customers now take for granted - day after day. This is both difficult and, therefore, often a major source of sustainable competitive advantage. Secondly, the brand promise mustn't become a straitjacket or too rigid: as we've seen for Tide, brands need to develop over time to promise and deliver additional benefits. Crucially, however, these are all related to the core brand promise and would be of little value if it stopped being reliably delivered. For the other two brands:

- Research Now's success is based on being tightly focused on the brand promise, but other benefits include outstanding client service, client staff training, and technical support for a range of different research methodologies (online diaries, conjoint studies, advertising testing, etc.) and markets (automotive, B2B, financial, healthcare).
- Aggreko continually reexamines the entire value chain to see how to improve the customer experience. Bruce Pool in the case study focused his initial response on customer service enhancements. The company has also used systems enhancements to give its field representatives better information about inventory availability, enabling reliable, market-leading response times. Aggreko has further enhanced its offer to assume total responsibility for power and temperature control at events – not just delivering and installing hardware. Finally it launched Aggreko Process Services, a consultancy aimed at improving the effectiveness and efficiency of any process operation challenged by environmentally adverse circumstances. The value proposition is again better operations, not 'kit'.

The Nokia case is more difficult. Its clear focus on *'Connecting people'* helped it overtake Motorola (which lacked focus) but the core benefit it promised is increasingly just part of what customers value. Nokia has built up an extensive range of products aimed at different segments and applications, but given the scale of what Apple and Google are now offering, it will need to refocus on benefits and global segments that are relevant to today's market while still building on its considerable sources of continuing competitive advantage.

Focus applies at the corporate as well as the brand level. A key part of Nokia's success came from the 1992 decision to concentrate 100% on telecommunications, with particular emphasis on digital mobile. In contrast, Motorola lacked corporate, as well as brand, focus. Research Now and Aggreko, too, are highly focused at the corporate level (and, unlike Nokia, always have been).

Even P&G, which covers many markets, has become more focused, concentrating its efforts on a few big, profitable categories and, within these, a few big, profitable brands. In AG Lafley's words,

> 'Developing a strategy meant deciding which industries, geographies, core capabilities, and competencies to focus on. We also had to understand where growth was going to come from, having the right branded products and brand mix. As an example, we decided to shift the company's portfolio from two-thirds household products to one-half household and one-half personal, beauty, and healthcare.'[92]

P&G's culling of brand names is a big change from the historical situation. 20 years ago, it had ten competing brands in the US detergent market, each with a somewhat different brand promise and a separate brand management team and budget: Tide was still for extra-tough family laundry loads (*'Tide's in, dirt's out'*), Cheer was *'All-temperature'*, Gain, with a strong fragrance, was *'Bursting with freshness'*, Oxydol was for *'Sparkling whites – with color-safe bleach'*, and so on.[93] Today, P&G has only five brands in this market, each with numerous brand extensions.[94] Each brand may have a somewhat less clear positioning than before, but this is outweighed by the improved focus and efficiency of the overall business.

## The Range of Sources of Customer Insight

As we have stressed throughout, one of the key challenges of market-driving organic growth is the need to innovate aggressively, but only in ways that are relevant to the market. This is why we put so much stress on customer insights to guide innovation and resource allocation. Companies can learn about customers in many ways, some more 'high-tech', others more 'high-touch'.

More **high-tech** sources include:

- Quantitative market research: a wide range of techniques, increasingly using online data collection
- Customer database analysis to support evidence-based decisions about existing customers[95]
- Quantitative analysis of operational data, e.g. customer complaints, defections, response to price changes.

More **high-touch** sources include:

- Casual observation (e.g. of the way a manager's teenage children use technology)
- Direct customer contact ('immersion')
- Qualitative market research, increasingly including more sophisticated techniques such as metaphor elicitation
- Mystery shoppers (which can also generate quantitative data)
- Root cause analysis of individual critical incidents, complaints, customer defections, etc. (asking 'Why?' five times gets you deep into the root causes of problems)
- Learning from employees, especially customer-facing staff (discussion groups, suggestion schemes, competitions); a recent addition to this is staff monitoring, or directly engaging with, social media discussion of the brand, competitor brands, the category, and related issues.
- Small-scale pilot tests (fast prototyping)
- Market intelligence, e.g. learning from established competitors, new entrants, other industries, lead users.[96]

Not all of these are relevant to all companies, but few companies systematically use the full range of sources of insight which are available to them.

You may notice that we didn't mention focus groups among the recommended 'high touch' sources of insight. Focus groups are easy to organize and certainly generate insights, but they create a number of issues of group dynamics which reduce their efficiency and validity. Our general advice is to use semi-structured depth interviews rather than focus groups: for a given expenditure, these will usually give you more and better insights than focus groups because each interviewee has as much time as she needs and gives her answers independently of the rest.[97]

The one exception is that a focus group can be a good way of exploring peer relationships among people who know each other well such as a group of teenagers who hang around together - or the friends of the women in the Tide advertising research. Even in these cases, however, you need to be aware of people's tendency to adopt a particular persona within the group and to self-censor some of what they say.

In addition to the sources of customer insights listed above, the explosive growth of social media provides some powerful new ways of learning about customers.

### *Insights from social media*[98]

Much of the excitement about social media focuses on their role in marketing communications - brilliant when they succeed (as with Blendtec's 'Will it blend?' campaign, discussed in Chapter 2) but much less important to most companies than using social media to generate rich, unmediated, customer insights. These can be both high-touch (online discussion groups, customer advisory panels and brand communities) and, increasingly, high-tech (monitoring and analysis of large-scale social media data). Facebook in particular has such huge reach that it can provide detailed quantitative analyses of communication flows between consumers. Increasingly smart natural-language-processing technology will, over time, help marketers extract further insights from the content of those discussions.

The high-tech opportunities from social media are still developing but most companies have cottoned on to the high-touch ones, using these media for engagement and collaboration. Marketers at leading companies have created lively exchanges with and among customers on sites such as OPEN Forum (American Express), Beinggirl.com (P&G), myPlanNet (Cisco), and Fiesta Movement (Ford), tapping into participants' expertise and creativity for product development.

All P&G's businesses have sites aimed at specific markets and communities. Its feminine care group, appreciating the need to listen to rather than talk at consumers, made sure that Beinggirl was less about its products than about the trials and tribulations of being an 11-to-14-year-old girl - embarrassing moments, hygiene concerns, boy trouble. Its main value to P&G is not that it drives product sales but that it illuminates the target consumers' world.

Similarly, Amex uses OPEN Forum to learn about small business owners, and Cisco uses myPlanNet to help it understand the new generation of developers. These sites work because participants are engaged with the brands, find the platforms authentic, and trust one another. The companies create active communities by ceding some control - which in our experience is often the hardest adjustment for marketers.

The obvious danger with social media is failing to keep pace with developments. But an equal, less obvious danger is getting distracted by them and losing sight of the fundamentals. Keeping everything linked to the brand promise should help you avoid this pitfall. Consider Virgin Atlantic Airways (VAA).

### *Virgin Atlantic: using social media insights to buttress the brand*

Customers expect innovation, fun, informality, honesty, value, and a caring attitude from VAA. This promise is reinforced at every customer touch point, from marketing materials and the call center to travel agents and, increasingly, travel websites. VAA scans these sites to learn what people are saying. Where there is misinformation, it rarely has to provide a correction, because site visitors themselves usually do so. VAA uses the data to check that the brand promise is both understood and relevant. It also works to keep all its social media activities true to and in support of the brand values. For instance, the most-read section of its Facebook page includes travel tips from crew members - communication that comes across as honest, informal, and caring.

For VAA - and for most companies - the biggest social media opportunity lies in gathering insights to drive continuous improvement. For instance, when it learned that its loyalty-scheme members were complaining online about tedious, redundant requests for security information, it created a secure opt-in service to eliminate the problem. In response to other online-community suggestions, it launched a system to arrange taxi sharing on arrival with passengers from the same flight. None of this represents a shift in strategy: the brand promise hasn't changed, but social media dialogue has enabled VAA to keep improving its offer.

Again, Facebook interactions helped VAA appreciate an important but largely unrecognized segment: consumers planning a big trip. Their planning starts well in advance and involves extensive discussions with other travelers, so VAA launched V-Travelled, a site dedicated to inspirational journeys. Customers moderate the conversation and exchange information, stories, and advice. They can create a Trip Pod, a personal scrapbook of ideas for a dream trip. VAA enters the discussion using a traveler's tone of voice, not pushing a product but offering advice. V-Travelled does lead to some sales, but its main benefit to VAA comes from brand reinforcement and novel customer insights.

Other incremental innovations emerging from VAA's social networking include a loyalty scheme, Facebook Flight Status app (a first for any airline) and VAA's first iPhone app, called Flight Tracker, which includes real-time aircraft positions - also a first for any airline.

We now turn to two aspects of the crucial, and much misunderstood, relationship between customer insights and innovation. This relationship varies between different contexts, specifically:

- Different *types* of innovation, from strictly incremental to highly radical
- Different *stages* of innovation, from initial idea to introduction and beyond.

## Insights for Incremental versus Radical Innovation

The distinction between incremental and radical innovation is not clear-cut but the ways in which innovations vary along the continuum between the two is important. One difference is that both the *focus* and the *sources* of customer insight vary, depending on whether the innovation is relatively incremental or radical.

In terms of focus:

- As discussed in Chapter 3, your main initial focus should be on *understanding and reducing the drivers of customer dissatisfaction with your brand*. The role of customer insights here is to highlight where there is a problem and then provide data to enable diagnosis and remedial action.
- With this foundation, you should look for ways of driving the market by improving the brand promise ahead of current customer expectations (while still ensuring reliable delivery of the improved promise), the topic of this chapter. This means *increasing customers' positive satisfaction with the brand* relative to the current brand promise and the competition. Customer insights here are crucial to ensure relevance and successful execution.
- For the more radical types of innovation discussed in Chapter 5, the first aim is to uncover 'latent' market needs, which often means *discovering and understanding customers' unstated sources of dissatisfaction with the whole category.*

After that, the role of customer insights is again to ensure relevance and successful execution.

In other words, for these different types of innovation, you are trying to understand different things. In addition, as you move from reliably delivering the current offer to improving it incrementally and then more radically, the process shifts from being:

- Mainly *reactive* (responding to evidence of customer dissatisfaction) and *inward-looking* (improving operations to eliminate problems), to
- Mainly *proactive* (driving the market through innovation) and *outward-looking* (testing for customer relevance).

As a broad generalization, incremental innovation should be driven and kept relevant using the full range of high-tech and high-touch insight data. For more radical innovations, high-tech methods are less helpful and companies have to rely on high-touch methods, preferably including direct customer contact and small-scale pilot tests.

## Different Stages of the Innovation Process

Every innovation, however large or small, incremental or radical, pioneering or following, goes through a broadly similar set of stages, although the details vary infinitely. The following represents a fairly typical process, albeit considerably idealized (in practice, the process is always much messier, with numerous stops and starts, dead ends, iterations, etc - as with the initial development of Tide):

1. Initial idea
2. Development
3. Piloting/prototyping

4. Introduction
5. Post-evaluation and longer-term continuous improvement

A customer insight can be important at every stage. Sometimes, it provides the initial idea (Step 1). But usually, the role of customer insights throughout the process is to test the proposed innovation - often, alternative options - for customer relevance in order to help management decide whether to proceed to the next stage and, if so, how to improve the proposal.

The improvement aspect is sometimes underestimated. For instance, people tend to assume that the classic test market is to enable management to make a 'go/no go' decision about a new product. In reality, it may be just as much about developing the marketing mix for the launch, perhaps by testing different combinations of price and promotion, as well as getting trade and consumer responses to the product, advertising, etc.

Increasingly, companies are using fast prototyping to get consumer responses which are more reliable than attitude surveys and much faster, cheaper, and more commercially confidential than traditional test markets. A fast prototype does not need to be a fully realistic representation of what the product/service will be if launched; it just needs to be good enough to generate sufficiently reliable customer responses for management purposes.[99]

The increasing use of fast prototyping reflects a number of interrelated shifts:

- Increasing emphasis on speed, reinforced by the growth of the internet
- A move towards testing ideas 'for real' rather than trying to predict the level of consumer uptake using rationalistic concept tests etc., which are inherently unreliable. This parallels the long-term shift towards direct, especially internet-based, marketing communications: what matters is often simply which execution works, not why, or whether we could have predicted it

- A feeling that lengthy stage-gate processes - where a proposal has to cross a long series of hurdles - can be bureaucratic and too cautious: they give the nay-sayers (or 'tooth-suckers') too many chances to stop an idea from reaching the market.

The problems of a stage-gate model are especially marked for more radical innovations. Bold ideas - which may be very good or very bad - are more likely to get screened out than more conventional ideas.

## Summary

The issues discussed in this chapter lie at the heart of market-driving organic growth. The Tide story exemplified the approach:

- Its launch in 1946 was a genuine successful breakthrough innovation (i.e. both radical and pioneering)
- The hidden foundation of its extraordinary continuing success has been reliable delivery of the brand promise to both trade customers and consumers
- Building on that foundation, the main driver of its growth has been the repeated improvement and extension of that promise through continuous incremental innovation (some of which would be seen within the business as quite radical, including some brand extensions and the recent US advertising campaign)
- Rigorous use of a wide range of consumer insights to ensure continuing relevance, with increasing emphasis on immersive approaches and the 'whole' consumer
- Strong leadership and values, driving and supporting all of the above.

In the rest of the chapter, we further explored the idea of relentless, incremental innovation, supported by customer insights to ensure continuing relevance. We specifically discussed four generic issues:

- The need for ambition and focus
- The range of sources of customer insight, including social media
- Insights for incremental versus radical innovation
- The role of customer insights at different stages of the innovation process.

**Idea Check**

***1. Are you the best – from a customer perspective?***
Recheck your espoused vision for superlatives. Are you offering the most or least, newest or oldest, biggest or smallest, fastest or slowest, the finest, greatest, sharpest, or just the best? Really? Do you have credible evidence that your customers agree with you? Excellent! Be ready to prove these claims. If you can't claim the position you should figure out what it would take to do so. You need to be demonstrably best on the total value to your target market. When you can claim it, be assured that your direct competitors are coming after you, studying everything you do with intent. If you stand still they will catch you. Be ambitious: to achieve continuing, market-leading growth, raising the promise bar is a necessity, not an option. It is never impossible. Nor is it a one-off event. Market-leading companies are not relaxing places to work: exhilarating but obsessive, relentlessly looking for improvement in a never-ending process.
***2. Are you focused?***
Once more, without power points: What business are you in? What's your strategy? What's your primary brand promise? Examine growth over the last 5–10 years. Where did it come from? Has it caused you to lose focus? If you have to think hard (or really think at all) to reconcile your growth initiatives with your team's shared and enduring sense of your strategy, you've lost focus. Not a winning position.

***3. Are you aligned?***

When was the last time you were surprised and fired up by a customer insight? Not all are exciting to managers but the potential to enhance the customer's experience should enthuse and engage you and your team. Invest in effective communication. Communication isn't just about getting the data in front of the decision makers. It is about sharing emotion and passion. You need to rise to the challenge of moving your internal audience, mobilizing the energy inside.

# CHAPTER FIVE

# INNOVATING BEYOND THE FAMILIAR

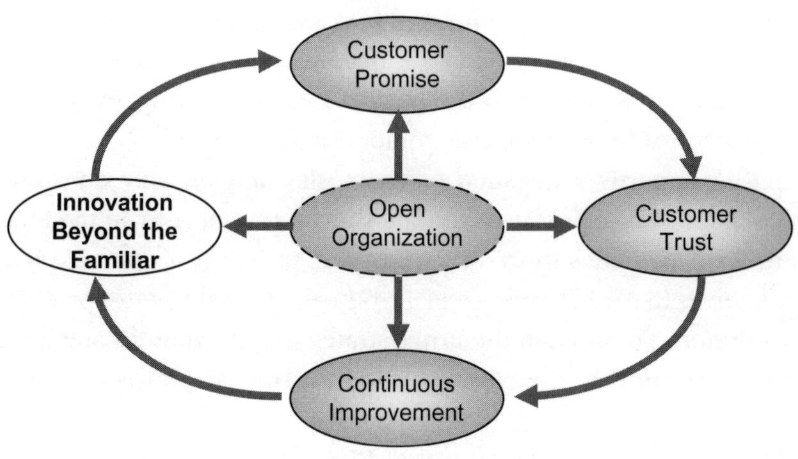


'*The word innovation has become overused, clichéd, and meaningless*'.

– Andy Grove, Former Chairman of Intel[100]

'Overused and clichéd'? – yes. 'Meaningless'? – not at all. Innovating 'beyond the familiar', the topic of this chapter, is in some ways the high point of our journey in this book. It is neither an alternative to the other stages of the journey nor an optional extra. Having a clear, relevant customer promise, reliably delivering it to build trust and brand equity, and continuously improving it are all essential, but in the long run, they are unlikely to be enough to ensure sustained, market-driving profit growth. Companies must also have the courage to go further.

In discussing this topic, however, we need to cut through a lot of distracting and even misleading nonsense and focus on what matters: how to ensure that the company doesn't stay too much within its comfort zone and then how to manage the risks when it ventures further. These risks increase disproportionately with the amount of change involved, especially on the demand side (innovations that involve big changes in customer behavior are always risky) and even more for the first mover in a new-to-the-world category. Even for later entrants to a category, when customer needs and how to meet them are becoming clearer, going too far beyond what is familiar to the business means moving away from its sources of knowledge and competitive advantage.

Risk is partly a question of timescale. Relying only on incremental innovation is low-risk in the short term but risky in the long term as it becomes more likely that a competitor – quite likely a newcomer to the industry – will introduce a radically better product or solution. To broaden the firm's strategic opportunities and limit this long-term risk, the killer question for this chapter is:

**'Have you embraced any novel ideas that have produced significant innovations beyond the familiar during the past three years?'**

Truth to tell, few companies can honestly answer yes to this question if by 'significant' we mean a really new product, process, service, target market, or business model important enough to make a big difference (at least, say, 15 or 20%) to the long-term bottom line. The first task at this point is therefore to ensure that the company has the ambition, restlessness, paranoia, curiosity, openness, humility, and ruthlessness to go beyond incremental improvements and actively search for new threats and opportunities with the aim of adapting to them or exploiting them ahead of the competition. In this context, companies should still generally aim to be the first mover, while never being too proud to imitate a competitor that introduces something better for customers.

There is a limit to this argument, however. Crucially, and contrary to much of the rhetoric about innovation, the best risk-adjusted opportunities are rarely in completely new markets which involve radical change for suppliers and customers. Instead, this chapter is mostly about innovating into 'adjacent' areas: beyond the incremental but *related to and building on* the company's existing business.

In reality, successful innovation by established companies almost always exploits existing assets and competitive advantages and involves much that is already familiar on the supply side and/or the demand side. In contrast, heroic 'blue sky' pioneering innovation into an area where the business has no knowledge or competitive advantage is like gambling shareholders' money at the casino: great when it works but more likely to end in tears. In fact, as we'll discuss – and despite much well-known advice to the contrary – the evidence is that for 'really new' markets and technologies, the best strategy is usually to be a fast follower, not the pioneer.

To illustrate what we mean, let's look again at Apple, currently the exemplar of innovation *Beyond the Familiar*. You've doubtless read and heard plenty about Apple but much of this is, we think, misleading in two important ways: first, it often mistakenly presents Apple as a pioneer in new product categories rather than a fast follower; secondly, it ignores the amount of unglamorous incremental innovation work behind the razzmatazz of the headlines and the big product launches.

## Apple – the World's Leading Innovator

No-one disputes Apple's ability to develop and launch innovative products that delight customers, outflank competitors, and transform industries: it is widely regarded as the most innovative company in the world.[101] Since CEO Steve Jobs rejoined in 1997 its financial performance has been extraordinary: By May 2010 Apple had passed Microsoft to become the second largest US corporation, ranked by market capitalization.[102]

The Apple brand inspires a level of devotion unique among big technology companies. Some people see this as just an emotional response to its clever positioning as a plucky challenger to IBM and then Microsoft, or the stylishness of its products, stores, and product launches. There's something in this view, but it ignores one other astonishing fact: Apple's consistently high customer satisfaction. Its ACSI score of 86 is *nine points higher than that of its nearest competitor* in the computer industry. No other company in the ACSI leads its industry by such a wide margin.[103] To achieve this dominance, Apple works its socks off on execution, delivering the brand promise reliably day after day and continuously improving it year after year. This doesn't grab many headlines, but provides the foundation for all the glamorous stories that do.

In reality, when Apple enters new (to the company) categories, it does so not as a pioneer but as a 'user-centric fast follower'. (The main exception, the Apple Newton personal digital assistant, failed, as we'll discuss). There were plenty of portable digital music players before the iPod in 2001. iTunes (2003) was not the first online music store. Apple wasn't even the first to recognize the potential of providing an integrated music offering. The iPhone was not the first smart-phone, nor the iPad the first tablet computer. Yet Apple has repeatedly gone on to dominate these markets with premium-priced high-end offers which combine features and capabilities initially developed by others, backed by solid investments in brand communications, product and service design and innovation, and world-class execution.

All these products have benefited from the Apple brand and further reinforced it, boosting sales of the other products and again illustrating the two-way relationship between brand and innovation. The brand was first established beyond electronics hobbyists with the 1977 Apple II personal computer, but it was the 1984 Apple Mac that turned it into a global icon. The Mac exemplifies Apple's approach to innovation *Beyond The Familiar*.

### *Apple as a user-centric fast follower: the Apple Mac story*

It is well known that the Graphical User Interface (GUI) and other key personal computing technologies such as the mouse, laser printing, and the Ethernet local area network protocol were first developed at Xerox's legendary Palo Alto Research Center (PARC).[104] Steve Jobs visited PARC in 1979, saw a working prototype with a GUI, immediately realized how this could transform the PC user experience, and rushed back to Apple to develop what eventually became the Mac.

Xerox did launch a product based on the PARC technologies – three years before the Apple Mac. The 1981 Xerox Star[105] had a GUI, icons, folders, mouse, built-in Ethernet, email, and a scanning laser printer. Xerox had all the tangible ingredients for market success: world-beating technology, deep pockets, a strong global brand, extensive manufacturing and supply chain capability, and a huge, well-established sales and service network. But it saw Star as a networked 'office of the future' system for document preparation, aimed at its traditional customer base of office managers in large organizations. It never went *Beyond The Familiar*, never made the effort to understand end users. Star flopped. According to Jobs,

> 'Basically they were copier heads that just had no clue about a computer and what it could do. And so they just grabbed defeat from the greatest victory in the computer industry. Xerox could have owned the entire computer industry today. … Could have been the IBM of the nineties. Could have been the Microsoft'.[106]

Apple didn't get it right first time either. Its first GUI-based PC, the Lisa (1983), was slow and, at $9,995, hugely overpriced. Its potential market at that price was tiny, so software suppliers refused to develop applications for it. Like Star, it flopped, despite market-leading features and a typically brilliant launch presentation.

Learning from the failure of Lisa, however, Apple threw its effort into the rapid development of the Mac and its spectacular 1984 launch which, according to the lead copywriter Steve Hayden, sought to position it as *'... the computer for the rest of us'*.[107] The Mac's high price and lack of system compatibility (Apple refused to license the technology) prevented it from becoming the standard and its huge development and launch costs and slow initial sales almost bankrupted the company. Nevertheless, it firmly established Apple in the post-PARC personal computer space, differentiated on the dimension of user-friendliness:

> 'The gold standard now for personal electronics is, "Is it easy enough for my grandmother to use it?" People on the Macintosh project were the first people to talk about a product in that way'.
>
> – Alex Soojung-Kim Pang, Research Director, Institute for the Future.[108]

Note that, with the Mac, Apple:

- Did not invent the key technologies – it copied them from PARC and then added numerous minor improvements.
- Was not the pioneer: Lisa launched two years after the Xerox Star.
- Did not succeed first time. It learned from Lisa's failure and quickly followed up with a much better offer, the Mac.
- Has introduced a continuing stream of new Mac products over more than 25 years, all based on incremental innovation, including today's iMacs, MacMinis, and MacBooks.

The last point reflects the other under-appreciated aspect of Apple: having entered a new (to the company) market as a user-centric fast follower, it then enthusiastically embraces incremental improvement.

### *Apple's relentless incremental innovation*

Apple's early iPods were beset with problems, which shook consumer confidence, but it quickly introduced improved versions, expanded into closely related services such as music downloads and movie rentals, and added a range of better and cheaper variants such as the 'shuffle', the 'nano', and the 'touch'. By the end of 2010 the iPod family of products and services, including iTunes, the iPhone and the iPad, accounted for 66% of Apple's total revenues.[109]

Apple's latest product, the iPad, follows the pattern. It is certainly not the first tablet computer: its aim is instead, through better execution, to be the first to achieve large-scale adoption and usage. Again, a safe prediction is that Apple will aggressively follow up with incrementally improved versions and a growing number of applications (including many shared with the iPhone) aimed at making the iPad the dominant force in the growing market for portable electronic media consumption.

In all these examples, much of Apple's success comes from its rare ability to translate deep understanding of the user experience – its frustrations as well as its aspirations – into products that work reliably and intuitively and are a pleasure to use. This is not done without effort. In Steve Jobs's own words:

> 'I get asked a lot why Apple's customers are so loyal. It's because when you buy our products, and three months later you get stuck on something, you quickly figure out [how to get past it]. And you think, "Wow, someone over there at Apple actually thought of this!" And then three months later you try to do something you hadn't tried before, and it works, and you think "Hey, they thought of that, too." And then six months later it happens again. There's almost no product in the world that you have

> that experience with, but you have it with a Mac. And you have it with an iPod'. [110]

How come *'Someone over there at Apple actually thought of this'*? Simple! The folks at Apple always try to walk in the end-users' shoes and relentlessly sweat the details. They try things out, make mistakes, learn and improve, fast but incrementally. Apple has managed to reduce the 'empathy gap' with users much better than most technology companies, but it also lives and breathes Edison's famous maxim about genius being 1% inspiration and 99% perspiration. The 1% inspiration is an essential part of its DNA which few other companies can match, but so is the 99%: it aims to be creative *and* user-focused *and* obsessive about execution.

### *Apple makes a small number of big bets*

To execute so well, Apple concentrates its resources on a limited number of products:

> 'Too many companies spread themselves thin, making a profusion of products to defuse risk, so they get mired in the mediocre. Apple's approach is to put every resource it has behind just a few products and make them exceedingly well'.
>
> – Tim Cook, COO, Apple[111]

One consequence is that bets tend to be big, requiring high risk tolerance and an acceptance that there will be painful failures. In 1993, after extensive and expensive market research and product development, Apple launched the Newton, a revolutionary Personal Digital Assistant (PDA) closely associated with CEO John Sculley. But the Newton did not deliver on the brand promise. Its widely publicized handwriting recognition, although better than on any previous mass market product, fell below customer expectations and sales failed to reach target levels. Eventually, left for dust by the much superior Palm Pilot, the Newton was withdrawn in 1998 although some of its technology contributed to the later success of the iPhone.[112]

Other Apple failures include the Pippin games machine (1995) and the G4 Cube desktop (2000). The Apple TV digital media receiver, launched in 2007, still hasn't gained real market traction. The company claims to see its potential and continues to invest. It accepts setbacks like these as part of the innovation game. As a general rule, and the Newton aside, Apple has been adept at quickly learning from its failures - as with Lisa in 1983 - and moving on.

Despite these occasional setbacks, Apple has successfully disrupted several previously unrelated industries: personal computing, music, movies, and smart-phones have all felt its influence. Television, video games, print publishing, and others may yet do so. In this sense, Apple is indeed a revolutionary company. Yet it is rarely a radical pioneer: apart from the Newton, which was launched under John Sculley and failed, its products do not use new-to-the-world core technology nor are they even category pioneers. Instead, we have described it as a user-centric fast follower and a relentless incremental improver.

## Innovating Beyond the Familiar: the Broader Lessons

No-one knows how long Apple will manage to keep hitting the sweet spot - it failed to keep its eye on the ball a few times lately and is now facing new left-field competition from Google and others, as well as from traditional competitors. Nevertheless, every company can learn from it, although many learn the wrong - or at least, only some of the right - lessons. Some of these are about the issues discussed in the previous chapters. Apple's brand promise is clear, relevant and emotionally compelling; the focus on meeting user needs is part of its DNA; its delivery is usually impeccable; and it relentlessly invests in fast incremental improvement.[113] But of course it has also been extremely good at pushing the boundaries while remaining customer-focused - the theme of this chapter.

In the rest of the chapter we discuss the evidence and advice for companies more generally:

- Why and how you need to look beyond your comfort zone for potential new threats and opportunities (as Xerox did only half-heartedly)
- Why you should aim to be the first to exploit opportunities in areas adjacent to your current capabilities and markets: most of the best (risk adjusted) "beyond the familiar" opportunities are in these areas
- How to manage the inevitable risks of adjacent innovation
- Why, for new-to-the-world categories, you should generally aim to be a fast follower that executes boldly and well, like Apple, rather than the category pioneer.

## Why and How You Need to Look Beyond Your Comfort Zone

When a disruptive new technology or competitor appears from nowhere, like Apple and Google bursting into the mobile handset market, established players like Nokia obviously need to respond urgently, almost certainly going outside their strategic comfort zone. Similarly, The Mobile Channel, featured in Chapter 2, had no choice: simply to survive, it had to change its business model, from permission-based mobile advertising to online market research (re-branding as Research Now).

Usually, however, new threats and opportunities creep up less obtrusively. In the last chapter, we saw how Tide's consumer research showed that, despite relentless and successful incremental product innovation, the brand was slowly losing its perceived relevance to most American women. To counter this, the brand team had to develop a radical new advertising strategy.

### *What if there's no 'clear and present danger'?*

Absent the impetus from a 'clear and present danger,' top management may still be able to use evidence of a credible *potential* threat (e.g. from a new technology, competitor, or regulatory enquiry) to reduce complacency and force more radical thinking.

But even where there is no easily identifiable danger, you should make the effort to look for new threats and opportunities beyond the horizon to overcome inertia and complacency. In the words of the Wharton School's George Day, there is almost always a bias towards 'Safer, incremental line extensions and product improvements' due to factors such as:

- *Tunnel vision*: missing the early, weak signals of new threats and opportunities at the periphery
- *Exploitation versus exploration*: an exclusive focus on business process improvements, efficiency and reliability drives companies to ignore new, bold opportunities
- *Short-termism*: financial pressures create an undue preference for quick-payback, low-risk projects
- *Resource constraints*: because of constant pressure on time and resources, the urgent tends to squeeze out the important.[114]

The tendency to stay within the firm's comfort zone is greatest when the business is doing well and there are no obvious storm clouds in the sky. To counter it, George Day and Paul Shoemaker recommend firms to ask themselves, systematically, questions such as: *What have been our past blind spots?, What are the mavericks and trouble-makers within the company trying to tell us?*, and *What future surprises could really hurt us - or help us?*.[115]

### *Ideas from lead users and other markets*

Another leading scholar in this area is Eric Von Hippel at MIT, who pioneered the benefits of learning from lead users and unfamiliar usage contexts, that is, new, extreme, or unusual customer problems and how people are already solving them. He defines lead users as, *'Those organizations (individuals) facing needs early, and positioned to benefit significantly by obtaining a solution to those needs.*[116] Especially in B2B markets, some customers are repeatedly ahead of their competitors in adopting new products and processes. To find novel opportunities beyond the familiar, talk to these leading-edge customers about their longer-term aims, the capabilities they will need to build and the problems they will need to solve to achieve them, and how your company might help.

Von Hippel cites the example of Keller Tool's solder-less wrapped connection equipment. Keller was commissioned by Western Electric - a classic lead user - to develop and manufacture a new system because there was no available solution on the market. As well as profitably supplying the system to Western, Keller also sold it to other companies - who until then had not realized they could use anything like it: neither they nor Keller had spotted the opportunity.

3M, with classic successes such as Post-It notes, Scotch tape, and Thinsulate, is a renowned innovator and a keen user of Von Hippel's thinking. For example, it combined insights from battle-field surgeons (who place a high premium on speed) and make-up artists (who have found many ways to attach different materials to skin) to develop a patient infection control product which then formed the basis of long-term strategy for its Medical-Surgical business.[117]

## *'Co-creation' and open innovation*

A somewhat similar process, 'co-creation', involves inviting existing customers - not necessarily lead customers - of companies such as Lego and PepsiCo to participate in new product development. Where this differs from Von Hippel's approach is that co-creation with mainstream users is typically more about more incremental innovations, such as new potato chip flavors at PepsiCo's UK company Walkers.[118] Somewhat similar thinking - tapping into customers' creativity - underlies the iPhone App Store and customization services such as Nike's NIKEiD shoe store.

The co-creation mentality also applies to 'open' research and innovation. R&D-driven organic growth has long been a priority at P&G, but in 2000 incoming CEO AG Lafley challenged its proud 'invented here' culture, initiating a new era with *'Connect and Develop'* (C&D).[119] Lafley's mandate was to get the company to a point where half of its new products were coming from its R&D labs and half from outside. This called for collaboration with organizations and individuals around the world. Networks created or harnessed include:

- Nine Sigma, a broker which accesses 700 000 scientists and technologists, inviting them to solve problems posed by P&G
- InnoCentive, 70 000 contract scientists, similar but more suited to when the scientific or technical problem posed is fairly well structured, and the solution is likely to come from a narrow field or discipline, and
- YourEncore, a network of 800 top retired R&D scientists, established by P&G but now independent: any company can hire members to work as daily consultants.

C&D has been a big success. By 2006, 35% of new products had elements originating from outside the company (up from 15% in 2000). C&D successes include Olay Regenerist, Swiffer Dusters and the Crest SpinBrush. These innovations were enabled by important technical breakthroughs and commercialized by leveraging and enhancing existing P&G brands.[120]

### *Radically improving - or eliminating - service features*

Most of these examples are for products, not services. In service markets, another strategy for going beyond the familiar is to ask which of the generally accepted parts of the offer could be either dramatically improved or omitted altogether. An example of the first type is Cemex's promise of same-day on-site cement delivery within twenty minutes of the specified time.[121] A classic example of the second is Southwest Airlines' pioneering 'no frills' concept, further developed by European operators such as Ryanair and easyJet.

A key argument here is that, to achieve a low-cost offering with a clear advantage in simplicity and cost, you should aim to drop some service features altogether, e.g. no free in-flight meal rather than a nasty free meal that costs the airline 20% less than the competition's. To achieve a dramatically lower cost, the whole business system must be rethought: for instance, low-cost airlines need to achieve very high load factors and very fast turn-rounds. Of course, your marketing communications must then ensure that customers know what to expect – if they want to eat during the flight they must bring their own meal or buy one from your cabin staff. Provided the resulting low-cost promise is attractive to enough customers and is clearly communicated (to manage expectations), the evidence from the best low-cost airlines and other low-cost businesses such as Wal-Mart, Canon copiers (versus Xerox), and Ikea is that customer satisfaction and loyalty can be very high.

The best-known advocates of this approach are W. Chan Kim and Renée Maubourgne, authors of the best-selling book *Blue Ocean Strategy*. They propose value curve analysis (VCA) to help managers focus on what really matters to customers. VCA fights complacency and encourages achievable ambition (for example, identifying where service and delivery standards can be raised well above the industry norm) and reduces distraction and costs (by dropping attributes most buyers don't need and don't wish to pay for).

### *Beyond the familiar planning process*

Because of the numerous organizational and psychological forces discouraging firms from looking for threats and opportunities beyond their comfort zones, you need to boost this capability artificially through occasional events away from day-to-day pressures, typically off-site and externally facilitated to ensure open-ended challenge and discussion. Don't try to link this to existing plans, budgets or resource allocation, all of which are inherently political and start from the status quo. Instead, the workshop results should be selectively followed up by ad hoc task forces. Ideas that prove worth while will eventually find their way into the mainstream planning and budgeting system.

## Focus on Adjacencies

P&G defines innovation as everything that improves the value consumers get from putting their trust in its brands. It avoids making an arbitrary split into incremental and radical innovation. Unfortunately, much of the discussion of innovation assumes a clear-cut difference between these. In reality, this distinction is a matter of degree.[122]

This is not just an academic point - it has important practical implications. As the unfamiliarity of an innovation increases (for the industry, the firm, and its customers), the risks increase disproportionately. Moving away from what the firm knows and its sources of competitive advantage introduces unknown unknowns on top of the known unknowns. Further, there is evidence that demand-side risk (uncertainty about customer value) tends to be even higher than supply-side risk (uncertainty about whether the industry/firm can deliver at an acceptable cost) although there are many exceptions.

The practical implication is that, on a risk-adjusted basis, the main innovation opportunities beyond incremental improvement are in adjacent markets rather than new-to-the-world markets that represent a major discontinuity, especially in customer behaviour.[123]

### *The 'GE innovation portfolio'*

One company that systematically focuses on innovating beyond the familiar into adjacent areas is General Electric. Like P&G, GE rejects the idea that innovation is either incremental or radical.

Figure 5.1: GE's Innovation Portfolio

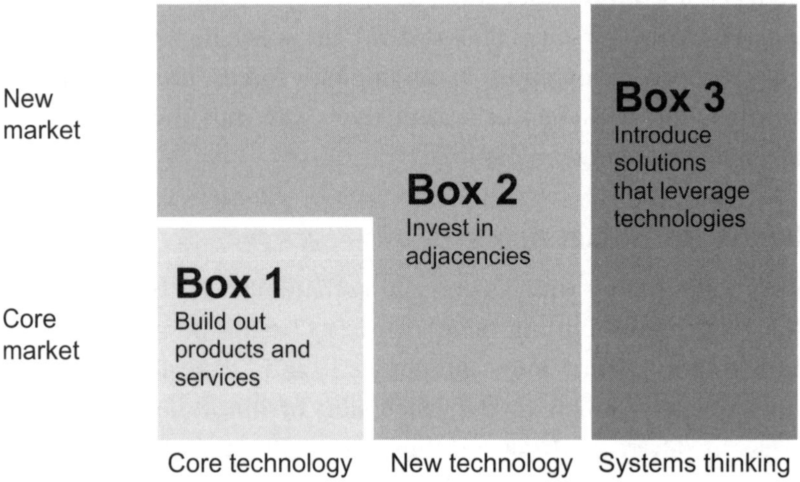

Instead, it maps opportunities against two dimensions: technologies and markets. It labels technologies as core, new, or systems, and markets as core and new, while accepting that these are fuzzy distinctions (Figure 5.1).

As with all companies, much of GE's innovation is incremental (Box 1: core technology, core market) along the lines of Chapters 3 and 4 of this book. But its main innovation effort is in Box 2 (new technology and/or new market), sometimes referred to as the adjacency sweet spot. Beyond these, GE also looks selectively for opportunities in Box 3, representing new systems thinking aimed at both core and new markets. According to Anubhav Ranjan, Director of Strategic Marketing, the distinctions are as follows:

- **Box 1:** Core new product innovations. Fill the gaps with better products/services at more price points
- **Box 2:** Adjacencies. Launch and build adjacencies that leverage brand and distribution
- **Box 3:** Systems thinking. Problem solving on a bigger scale … ecosystem level.[124]

The development of GE's innovation portfolio is part of a broader transformation to strengthen the company's ability to generate more organic growth through closer collaboration with customers, a broadening of the agenda to include more commercial as well as technological innovation, and a more strategic role for the marketing function. Marketers are now tasked with challenging the status quo, suggesting novel customer solutions (such as some of those in Box 3) and leading many of the discussions on market segmentation, pricing, product priorities, and so on, as well as its traditional support roles in market research, lead generation, advertising and promotion.

GE remains a technology powerhouse, but is now aiming to use this expanded marketing capability to ensure that all its innovation efforts across all three boxes in Figure 5.1 are focused on creating customer, and therefore shareholder, value.[125]

### *Leveraging the brand*

One reason to focus on adjacencies rather than on areas where the company has no competitive advantage is so that, like GE, you can use your existing brand. As already noted, a strong brand reduces the cost and increases the chance of success for new products and services, which - provided they deliver the customer promise - then reinforce the parent brand. This works both for line extensions within the brand's current category and for brand extensions into new (to the brand) categories - but only up to a point. If the new product tries to stretch the brand too far, not only will it lack credibility, it may also dilute and weaken the parent brand. The alternative - creating a new brand - avoids these risks but greatly increases the launch and support costs of the new product.

Especially for luxury brands, brand equity can also be diluted or tarnished if the brand is used for cheap or inappropriate products, often through licensing deals without proper controls.[126] When a large tobacco company developed a Tiffany cigarette brand, Tiffany successfully argued that this would damage its brand

and the product was never launched (at least, under that brand name).

Brand extensions are most likely to be accepted by consumers if:

- The perceived quality of the parent brand is high
- There is a good perceived fit between the parent brand (and its current category and the firm) and the proposed extension (product and category) and, to a lesser extent,
- The extension is not regarded as too easy to create.[127]

The key issue is perceived fit - a measure of the extent to which consumers see the attributes of the brand and the proposed extension as consistent. A brand whose image is based on abstract attributes (prestige, style, durability) tends to be more extendible than one with strong associations with a particular category or product feature such as stain resistance or a savoury flavor (consumers won't buy sweet snacks sold under a brand associated with savoury snacks).[128] For example, Virgin is a highly elastic brand seen as fun, friendly, young at heart, a bit anti-establishment, and good value for money. This makes it extendible to a wide range of consumer product and - especially - service categories, but not to a premium priced offer in one of those categories. In contrast, the Levis brand is so strongly associated with jeans that the attempt to launch Levis Tailored Classics suits was a famous disaster.[129]

If a brand extension does succeed, it can change the associations of the parent brand. Part of the thinking behind Levis Tailored Classics was the rather implausible hope that it would broaden the brand, allowing the company to use it on a wider range of products. Similarly, Volkswagen thought that launching the VW Phaeton (a large, rather bland, formal luxury car) would extend the brand into new territory: buyers of big Mercedes cars. In contrast, Toyota deliberately created Lexus as a separate brand. Most Lexus buyers know that it is part of Toyota - which gives them confidence in its reliability - but the separate brand conveys prestige, exclusivity, and market-leading service.

The benefits, limits, and risks of using an existing brand reinforce the advantages of adjacent innovations, beyond the familiar but still exploiting the firm's sources of competitive advantage, of which the existing brand is one.

## How to Manage the Risks of Adjacent Innovation

*All* innovation is risky. Even innovating within a target market and a category you know well can be risky and market research can reduce but not eliminate that risk. For example, Mattel pioneered modern dolls for girls with Barbie in 1959 and consolidated its position with the introduction of her boyfriend Ken in 1961. In 1991, it introduced a minor line extension: a new, contemporary outfit for Ken known as 'Earring Magic Ken'. The result was a fiasco. The new doll, developed using focus groups of 9-year-old girls, became known as 'Gay Ken' and was adopted by the gay community, rejected by middle America, and withdrawn from the market amid protests from both groups. In this case, the risks came not from potential rejection by the target market but from unintended consequences among other consumers and citizens.[130]

Often, the main known unknowns are on the supply side. The initial development and launch of Tide involved numerous supply-side risks but, on the consumer side, P&G already knew that there would be a big demand for a product with greatly superior cleaning power. It didn't know quite how big the market would be, nor how much more consumers would pay for a better product, but these known unknowns were relatively minor and could themselves be reduced through market research.

Probably more often, the main risks are on the demand side. For instance, we have seen how an existing brand can be stretched some way beyond what is familiar to the customer, but only up to a point - and that point varies between brands (some being much more elastic than others) and involves subtle issues around perceived fit. Market research on customers' perceptions of the brand and whether they would see a particular extension as appropriate can again reduce but not eliminate this uncertainty.

As we saw in Chapter 4, the best way to research demand-side risks depends on how far the innovation aims to take customers 'beyond the familiar': the more radical the innovation, the less the company can use 'high-tech' sources of insight, making it more reliant on 'high-touch' approaches and judgment.

## For New-to-the-World Categories, Be a Fast Follower

> 'It is better to be a follower than a pioneer. The pioneers get scalped'.
>
> - Andrew Carnegie, Robber Baron and Philanthropist[131]

Throughout this book, we have encouraged you to drive the market by relentlessly raising your game *ahead of the competition*. This holds for evolving the brand promise to keep it relevant, continuously improving the delivery of the promise and the offer itself, and introducing adjacent innovations 'beyond the familiar', as just discussed. What about really new - that is, new-to-the-world - products and services? Does the same apply? That is, for radical, new-to-the-world categories, should you also aim to be first to market?

Early research suggested that the answer is yes. The main evidence came from the 'order-of-entry effect', the correlation between market shares within established markets and the order in which the competing brands had launched. The brand or company that had been longest on the market had, on average, a higher market share than the one that had been second-longest on the market, and so on. Of course there was a lot of variation between markets, but there was a clear correlation between market shares and order of entry, suggesting a significant and long-lasting first-mover (or pioneer) advantage.[132]

People liked this conclusion, which encouraged bold, heroic innovation. Being a successful pioneer is hugely appealing: think of the fame and fortune achieved by companies such as FedEx, Southwest Airlines, Sony (with the Walkman), Dell, Starbucks, and Nintendo (with the Wii). What's not to like? Alas, these are exceptions. More recent research has shown that most of today's market leaders, often widely believed to be pioneers, were in fact fast followers, the actual pioneers having long since gone bust or exited the market. Pioneer advantage turned out to be largely a myth because the failure rate is so high. Note that, for the pioneer in a new-to-the-world category to succeed, all of four things must happen:

- Once launched, the new product or service must turn out to *meet a significant customer need*
- It must be possible to supply it at *a price enough customers are willing to pay* to make it profitable for at least one supplier
- You must be willing and able to *invest on a sufficient scale* both to create the market and to build a winning lead
- You must get the *execution* 'roughly right' first time and 'really right' before someone else (like P&G, Apple or Google) does so.

Given these four hurdles, it's hardly surprising that there are so few successful category pioneers.

### *Exploding the myth of pioneer advantage*

The key research exploding the myth of pioneer advantage in new categories was by Peter Golder and Gerard Tellis, who went back to uncover the actual early history of a wide range of categories.[133] Parallel work by Stephen Schnaars reached the same conclusions.[134] More recently, Constantinos Markides and Paul Geroski have shown how difficult it is for a radical pioneer – even if there's a real market opportunity – to build and maintain leadership in dynamically growing and changing markets. They specifically argue that the best strategy in new-to-the-world categories is usually to be a fast follower.[135]

The evidence from this research is that, with major new categories, the spoils most often fall to an early follower with a mass market perspective, willingness and ability to invest in scale, a focus on continuous improvement, and an existing customer base. The fast follower learns from the initial market response to the pioneer's offer, improves that offer, scales up production and distribution, reduces cost, and builds a dominant market share during the new category's critical early growth phase, which it also helps to drive by investing in marketing as well as in distribution and production.

Once the successful fast follower has established market leadership, it should then aim to be first with incremental and adjacent innovations, as we've discussed throughout the book. A typical example is disposable diapers. The pioneer was Chux, but P&G came in as a (fairly) fast follower with Pampers and built a highly profitable dominant market share, which it has maintained through relentless continuous improvement over many years.

Despite the research evidence, the idea of being a pioneer has kept its allure, reinforced by books such as Kim and Maubourgne's *Blue Ocean Strategy*.[136] Kim and Maubourgne show that successful radical innovations are, on average, more profitable than successful incremental innovations but admit that, '*We don't have data on the hit rate of success of red and blue ocean initiatives*'. Neither do we, but pioneering a new category clearly, on average, involves higher investment than launching a line extension and is also much riskier. It's therefore hardly surprising that, *when they succeed*, 'blue ocean' innovations create a bigger (absolute) increase in revenue and profit. That certainly doesn't mean they're a better risk-adjusted investment than incremental or adjacent improvements. In reality, as we've seen, the evidence is the opposite.[137]

To us, the value of *Blue Ocean Strategy* is that it forcibly encourages managers to look for threats and, especially, opportunities beyond their strategic comfort zones. This is all to the good and the starting point for this chapter. We also agree that, for adjacent innovations that directly build on the firm's existing sources of competitive advantage (like GE's 'Box 2' innovations on page 108), you should generally aim to be first to market - while not being too proud to copy the competition's best ideas if they get there ahead of you. But for new-to-the-world categories, our advice does differ from that of *Blue Ocean Strategy*: in this context, the biggest rewards usually go to an early follower that executes boldly and better than the competition.

As we have seen with Apple, being a fast follower does not mean being unambitious or lacking innovation. Nor does it mean avoiding all significant risks. Consider Google, another successful fast follower. When Google launched in September 1998, at least three years after the emergence of commercial sites offering search, several well-established brands were fighting for market share but the clear leader was AltaVista.[138]

AltaVista's revenue model relied on display advertising, so its priority was stickiness not search. In contrast, Google's founders Larry Page and Sergey Brin saw that, for the user, a search engine should above all else be easy to use and enable her to find relevant sources quickly. Whichever search engine will get her to the answer quickest will become her first choice next time and the one she recommends to others, creating value for both her and, by bringing traffic, the top-ranked sites it lists (which, of course, forms the basis of Google's business model).

Google understood the benefit to the user of a simple, intuitive layout. Its home page was clean and uncluttered, stripped down to the point where, to many commentators, it looked naked: no news, no weather, no horoscopes, no banner ads, just a goofy logo in Romper Room colors and a search bar floating on an empty page. It was so simple your grandparents really could use it. To protect its ability to deliver on its user promise (the best search site), Google banned graphical banners and allowed only text-based ads, clearly separated from its own rankings. Its search engine was also significantly faster and better at finding the most relevant sites.

The result was a customer experience simply better than what users had become used to and a business model based on also meeting advertisers' needs better than either direct competitors such as AltaVista and Yahoo or established media such as print classified ads and reference books.

In our terms, the development and launch of Google was certainly innovation beyond the familiar – for users, the industry, and advertisers. But Google wasn't the first – or even the fifth – company to introduce internet search as an alternative to print media. Like Apple in several categories, it was a follower that came to dominate the category through better customer insight and execution.

## Conclusion: Do an Apple – Re-interpret 'Innovation' and Raise Your Ambition

Innovating *Beyond the Familiar* is neither an alternative to doing the basics nor an optional extra: in the long run, incremental innovation is unlikely to be enough to deliver market-leading organic growth and will probably be riskier than occasionally venturing beyond the familiar as discussed in this chapter. The first task is therefore to ensure that the company has the ambition and ability to search actively for new threats and opportunities over the horizon with the aim of adapting to them or exploiting them ahead of the competition.

In practice, and contrary to much popular advice, most of the best risk-adjusted opportunities beyond the familiar are in adjacent areas rather than in blue-sky areas such as new-to-the-world categories, where demand is unknown and the firm has few sources of competitive advantage. We discussed how GE now defines its 'innovation sweet spot' within this adjacent zone.

Every case is unique and the distinctions between incremental, adjacent, radical, and new-to-the-world are not clear-cut, but you should generally aim to be the first mover except in a completely new category, where the winner is usually a fast follower who builds a dominant market share during the early growth phase through heavy investment and superior execution and then maintains it through relentless continuous improvement. As we discussed, Apple has done this repeatedly. Other successful fast followers we mentioned include Pampers (P&G) and Google. There are dozens of other examples in the sources we have mentioned.

To drive both the basics and innovation beyond the familiar requires an open organization and outstanding leadership, the final requirement for profitable organic growth and the topic of the next, final, chapter.

**Idea Check**

If you are serious about organic growth, occasionally innovating beyond the familiar is a must.

***1. Are you ready to start?***

Most companies need to get their house in order before starting. Your company is probably not an exception. Pause, review the customer satisfaction and dissatisfaction data and the underlying diagnostics – get closure on all the open items. Do a Toyota! Drive the market by relentlessly improving the promise (while still reliably delivering it) so that your competitors cannot keep up. Then you'll be ready to move to the next level.

***2. Is there scope in your industry?***

Yes there is. Irrespective of how good your customer satisfaction scores are, there is always scope. There is no end to consumers' and businesses' appetite for help. Help in getting on with their number one concern, 'brand me'. For most businessmen for example, an extra night at home trumps another night on the road, even if spent in the very best hotel chain.

***3. Do you aspire to be in the same league as Apple or Google?***

You must. Don't be intimidated by the hype. Persistence, ambition, agility, and openness to learning from failure of self and others are central to success. These are within everyone's grasp.

***4. Do you know the known unknowns?***

With so much to gain, these are a key battleground. If winning here were easy, the unknown wouldn't stay unknown for long. Open up your organization to multiple sources of problem-solving. Develop your solution and get it out there. You won't get it right first time. Build on what you learn about the unknown and the solution. Fast, persistent, hypothesis-driven learning is the key.

***5. Are you trying to discover the unknown unknowns?***

Don't try too hard, avoid structure, just turn the idea tap on. Trust employees and customers to drive your idea machine.

CHAPTER SIX

# OPENING UP: WHAT LEADERS MUST DO

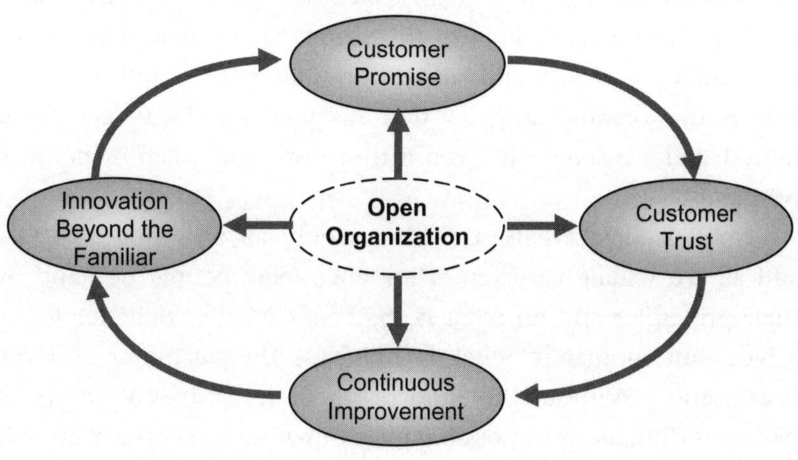


*'I don't want any yes-men around me. I want everybody to tell me the truth even if it costs them their job'*
– Legendary Hollywood Film Producer Samuel Goldwyn[139]

None of the things we have discussed so far – defining the promise, delivering it, improving it, innovating beyond the familiar – happen of their own accord. Someone has to make them happen. That someone is the organization's leader.

Think back to the cases we have looked at so far: in most, we can trace the impetus for action back to one, or a few, individuals such as Chris Havemann and Andrew Cooper at Research Now, Rupert Soames at Aggreko, AG Lafley at P&G, or Steve Jobs at Apple. It is not that these people sit and give directions or always plan personally what should be done (sometimes they do, sometimes they don't). What they all do, much more importantly, is give overall direction and create the climate for success, starting with the organization's values.

For better or worse, leaders embody these values. For successful *Beyond the Familiar* companies, the most powerful value of all is *openness*: openness to customers, so that their needs and wants are clearly and realistically understood, and openness within the organization, so that insights and ideas get transmitted and are acted on, even if they raise emotional or political problems.

Good leaders create a culture where all are willing to talk and all are willing to listen. They encourage people to stand by their principles and do what is right: not what is right for themselves, but ultimately what is right for the customer and the organization. Without this kind of open, values-based culture, it becomes difficult or impossible for companies to keep relentlessly delivering and improving the customer promise. The killer question for the chapter, which provides an acid test of the company's openness, is:

**'Have front-line staff asked you any uncomfortable questions or suggested any important improvements to your offering during the last three months?'.**

Few company leaders can honestly answer yes to this question – which means that most companies have the potential to become more open: this chapter is about how. Nevertheless, a few companies do come close to the ideal. Think back again to Research Now,

Aggreko, P&G, and Apple. An important part of their success has come from being better than their competitors at listening and learning from the market, reflecting their underlying values and the example set by its leaders.

Later in the chapter, we discuss the particular importance of open communication up the hierarchy; the corrosive influence of fear, which inhibits open communication; and two ways of reducing the problem: first, by rethinking customer and front-line contact programs, and secondly, by re-using 360-degree data for the specific purpose of opening up the organizational culture. Fundamentally, however, what matters most is the company's underlying values, as we now illustrate with Infosys, an extremely successful values-based company whose values come directly from its leadership.

## Infosys: 'Customer Delight' Beyond the Slogan[140]

When one of the authors, Patrick Barwise, joined IBM as a fresh-faced graduate trainee in 1968, the market for corporate information systems was dominated by IBM itself and by other, mostly US-based, mainframe suppliers such as Burroughs, GE, Honeywell, and RCA. People referred to *'IBM and the Seven Dwarfs'*.

Since then, the market has grown enormously and changed completely. Today, it is mainly about services and solutions consulting. A rejuvenated IBM leads again but the seven dwarfs are all different. Only two are American: Accenture and EDS. The rest are Indian technology companies that have become major global players in the last ten years such as Tata Consultancy Services and Wipro. The most widely admired of these new Indian kids on the block is Infosys.

Started in 1981 by seven software professionals in Bangalore, Infosys has increased its annual revenue from $9.5 million when it went public in 1993/4 to $4.8 billion in 2009/10, while maintaining an after-tax profit margin of over 28%, giving a remarkable CAGR of 47.5% for both revenue and income. Over the same period, its market capitalization has increased from $11 million to $39.5 billion. This sparkling performance has been achieved almost entirely through organic growth generated very much as proposed in this book: relentlessly increasing customer satisfaction and brand reputation through market-leading delivery performance. In an industry where only 75% of projects are delivered on time and on budget, the figure for Infosys is 94%.

Building on that foundation, Infosys has steadily raised its game by constantly adding value to the promise, while still ensuring its ability to deliver it. In the early 1980s, there were many companies acting as 'talent agencies' finding good Indian software engineers to work in the US for US clients, but Infosys was already focused on delivering project-based technology solutions. In the early days, these projects were relatively small and usually at the periphery of the customer's business. Through the 1990s, Infosys perfected its model of offshore software development: its salespeople sold software contracts in other countries and then shipped the work to be executed in Indian development centers. This model offered 80% lower costs because the Indian programmers worked in India instead of in the USA or Europe.

In 1999, Infosys established the Software Engineering and Technology Labs (SETLabs). The idea was to work with clients to help them enhance their own customers' experiences. SETLabs co-creates solutions with customers and other partners. It worked with BT on innovations such as rate-adaptive broadband speeds and simultaneous TV, gaming, video and music downloads. It helped a grocery chain which wanted to enable its customers to make healthier food choices via an ingredient healthiness rating system for almost 50 000 items: Infosys provided interfaces with the retailer's IT systems to make the information available for display, analysis, and procurement.

Vastly different from its start-up phase, Infosys now accommodates big projects central to its clients' businesses. Increasingly, these go beyond technology to incorporate the full range of client business activities. Already in 2003, Basab Pradhan, former head of worldwide sales, described how, *'Our selling pitch [used to be], "We have 100 Java engineers, and we can deliver for you from offshore. Now tell us what you want us to do." Today that is being replaced with, "We can give you a technical solution which will cut your inventory expenses by $100 million".'* [141] Today, Infosys is established as an end-to-end business transformation partner offering high-end consulting services, systems integration, and technology strategies, enabling it to emerge as a major player in the overall corporate IT services market.

### *Infosys: vision, mission, and values*

Fundamental to the success of Infosys is that it has a clear vision and mission and a strong, explicit set of corporate values and that it really puts these into practice. Its **Vision** and **Mission**, respectively, are:

- *'To be a globally respected corporation that provides best-of-breed business solutions, leveraging technology, delivered by best-in-class people'*
- *'To achieve our objectives in an environment of fairness, honesty, and courtesy towards our clients, employees, vendors and society at large.'*[142]

Amplifying these, its core **Values** are:

- *Customer Delight:* A commitment to surpassing our customers' expectations.
- *Leadership by Example:* A commitment to set standards in our business and transactions and be an exemplar for the industry and our own teams.
- *Integrity and Transparency:* A commitment to be ethical, sincere and open in our dealings.

- *Fairness:* A commitment to be objective and transaction-oriented, thereby earning trust and respect.
- *Pursuit of Excellence:* A commitment to strive relentlessly, to constantly improve ourselves, our teams, our services and products so as to become the best.

Many companies have official visions, missions, and values rather similar to these, but very few take them so seriously in their day-to-day business.

The most fundamental of the five values is the company's commitment to high ethical standards. In the words of chairman and co-founder Narayan Murthy,

> 'It is better to lose $100 million than a good night's sleep. And the softest pillow is a clear conscience. Never, ever do anything that is illegal or unethical, vis-à-vis society, competitors or customers.'[143]

Closely related is the commitment to surpassing customer expectations. Day to day, employees try to ensure that they understand the customer's needs, manage the customer's expectations, and reliably meet or exceed those expectations - when necessary, going the extra mile to deliver what was promised.

The impact of Infosys's values is shown most clearly on those occasions when it has turned down financially attractive opportunities which breach, or put at risk, these values. In these situations, actions speak much louder than words. Further, these stories are then retold within the company to demonstrate the values to new recruits.

### *How Infosys walked away from a $10 million contract*

In 2002, JB Ulrich [name disguised], a US multinational selling B2B products and services, was one of Infosys's top 20 global clients. It had grown quickly through a series of international acquisitions. Despite the global JBU brand, synergies were limited, with legacy management, systems, and processes. Fred Jackson, JBU's new corporate CIO, believed that standardizing the main client support application would provide significant competitive advantage with global clients. He proposed this to the board and received support, but on the basis that the project had to be funded by the country organizations.

With board-level backing, Fred developed an outline specification, a budget, and a broad-brush implementation plan with an aggressive nine-month timeline. Country heads agreed to fund the $10m project which was awarded to Infosys due to its track record with the company, knowledge of its existing systems, and appreciation of the complexity of the problem.

The project was launched in New York with a high-profile event. The Infosys team then got down to the detailed nuts-and-bolts planning. It soon emerged that Fred had not negotiated the new system functionality with even a sample of important users around the world. As he saw it:

- A team of corporate and Infosys engineers would visit each country to establish the precise functionality of its existing system.
- The team would then regroup at corporate headquarters, together with country representatives, to agree the functionality of the new global system.

Bharat Verma, the Infosys regional general manager, and his colleagues were enthusiastic about the potential business benefits for JBU from a global system but extremely worried by the project plan, especially since Fred was insisting that Infosys take total responsibility for delivering within his aggressive timeline. Based on their previous experience, the Infosys team felt that Fred's plan would be a recipe for endless discussion, with each country insisting on all the features of its existing application while minimizing the extent to which it changed its procedures. They proposed two changes to the project plan that they believed to be in the client's interest:

- Start the project with just two or three pilot countries to develop a system that would work for those countries and be an '80% solution' for the rest. This would provide a working framework against which the other countries could compare their own systems and debate which additional features would really be cost justified.
- Have someone with veto power: if a debate about functionality did not lead to a resolution reasonably quickly, someone should have the power to decide.

Fred was unwilling or unable to accept these changes. He did, however, suggest that JBU might share the project risk by allowing Infosys to charge any resource overrun on a cost-plus basis. This would have been financially attractive for Infosys but would not address the underlying problem which was organizational within the client, not technical: it could not be solved by deploying more technical resources.

Bharat and his colleagues felt that, if the client remained unwilling to accept their proposals to ensure successful implementation, the only option would be to reject the contract. He raised this with his boss Arvind Kumar, a main board member. Arvind fully supported him, feeling that the client would probably back down but if not, it would be best to walk away from the contract, despite the short-term pain and the risk to the much larger overall relationship with JBU.

In the event, JBU refused to accept Infosys's suggestions, took the contract back, and tried unsuccessfully to implement it itself using Fred's plan. After a year, the project was quietly dropped. Although the client was extremely upset with Infosys at the time, their relationship today is as strong as ever. The lesson? Infosys's values are not just words: in this case, the board member fully supported the team when it took a big short-term hit - walking away from a $10 million contract - rather than violating the company's values and putting at risk its precious reputation for reliable project delivery.

### *Bringing the values to life*

Infosys's espoused vision, mission, and values are brought to life not only through direct leadership from the top but also through employees' everyday actions. For instance, one key value is customer delight. In the words of co-chairman, Nandan Nilekani,

> 'At Infosys, we have a relentless focus on customer delight and every aspect of our operations centers around this mission. We have successfully endeavored to exceed client expectations by helping them become competitive in their marketplace.' [144]

Other values include leadership by example and the pursuit of excellence. Thus, throughout its development, Infosys has been unrelenting in its commitment to high quality standards in all aspects of its business. It aggressively pursues 'zero defects' and has achieved 9001:2008 certification and CMMI Level 5, a level reached by only 12% of companies tested. The same commitment to World Class led to Infosys being among the first Indian companies to adopt US GAAP financial reporting and the very first to list on an overseas stock exchange.

Infosys's values are mutually reinforcing. For instance, the emphasis on total customer satisfaction/zero defects helps top management make sure it keeps the whole organization customer-focused because code writers, as well as client managers, now get early contact with customers. More generally, Infosys's vision, mission, and values guide employees through inevitable dilemmas. When shared, accepted and understood, they allow everyone to see what does and does not fit.

## The Vital Flow: Open Communication Up the Hierarchy

Openness is the core value of all customer-focused, innovative companies. Successful customer-focused innovation depends on a firm's ability to generate valid, actionable information and insights about customers and competitors (as well as on technology, suppliers, and so on) and communicate this information to someone in a position to act on it. However, this alone is not enough. The message needs to be accepted and exploited, leading to an appropriate response - anything from a minor improvement to a breakthrough innovation. This applies whether the idea for the innovation comes from a new market insight, a new technology, or anywhere else - hence the importance of openness as a corporate value.

Three aspects of open communication in successful, innovative firms have already been widely recognized by both managers and researchers. Everyone knows that:

- **Visions, missions, values, and strategies need to be communicated down the hierarchy**. This is what top managers usually mean when they talk about the importance of communication. It is reflected in the first of our five killer questions: *'Can your middle managers accurately describe your customer promise?'*.
- **Effective management teams need to have open, fact-based discussion within the group** - in the words of Kathleen Eisenhardt at Stanford University, managers need to be able to *'argue but still get along'*.[145]
- **Innovative, market-oriented companies need to break down the silos** so that different functions and business units share customer insights and other information to ensure a timely and appropriate response to threats and opportunities in the market.[146]

What seems to be less widely recognized is that, in addition to open communication down the organization, within management teams, and horizontally between functions and units:

- Successful market orientation also requires **fearless vertical communication up the hierarchy**.

Not only is this last aspect largely unrecognized, it may also be the most important of the four, since it involves larger power differences (in the wrong direction) and therefore more fear, making it, by definition, harder to discuss openly.

### *The corrosive influence of fear*

In one - admittedly extreme - case, we met a consultant who had been commissioned by a large service business some years ago to investigate the reasons for its rapid market share loss to a cherry-picking competitor. The consultant analyzed existing market research and a sample of customer records. These showed, beyond reasonable doubt, that the company's aggressive price-cutting, although geographically targeted, was costing a fortune and having little impact on the loss of share. He proposed an alternative, value-added, strategy which would cost less and almost certainly work better.

However, when the client's market research manager, 'Alex', shared these important findings and proposals with her boss, whose strategy was shown to be costing the company so much money, the boss ordered her to remove them from her report, threatening repercussions on her career if she disobeyed. The analysis and proposed new strategy - which could have potentially saved the company tens of millions of dollars - never reached top management.

This happened several years ago. Alex's boss has left the company. Alex still works there but refused to meet us to discuss the incident. She is still afraid to talk about it, calling it a 'sensitive issue'.

People's unwillingness to discuss issues openly with their bosses occurs at all organizational levels. In fact, because senior managers have more to lose, they are often even more cautious about speaking up. In the words of one senior analyst, *'The options, the pension, everything is hanging on [not causing trouble]. I'm not going to jeopardize that.'* Everyone reports to someone. Even the CEO reports to the board and the board is itself accountable to shareholders, analysts, regulators, and the media. No one tells the whole truth.

The flow of bad news up the hierarchy is the oxygen of successful delivery and improvement. When something goes wrong with the product, service, or customer experience, the ideal is that those involved first make every effort to solve the problem (rather than walking away or blaming someone else or 'the system') and, secondly, tell their colleagues and bosses about it, perhaps with some initial thoughts on how things might be improved in the future.

When it works well, this process fuels the continuous incremental innovation at the heart of long-term performance in most businesses, from more reliable cars to friendlier banks to more accurate - and less incomprehensible - utility bills. Fear, however, silently destroys this type of non-stop bottom-up innovation. When that happens, the company's ability to deliver on, and relentlessly improve, its customer promise gradually weakens.

There's no great mystery about why people often don't communicate bad news or problems to their bosses. The main reason is simply that they don't want to get themselves or their colleagues into trouble or harm their career prospects. But less obviously, *people often don't even tell their bosses about positive improvement suggestions*. Why not?

- First, despite all the talk of engagement and empowerment, many employees are largely disengaged: they simply can't be bothered to go beyond what they've been told to do, especially if they resent the growing gap between average and top management remuneration.

- Second, they often feel that suggestions are a waste of time: if the management isn't listening, what's the point?
- Third, there may be peer pressure not to become a 'bosses' pet'.
- Finally, even a positive suggestion contains an implicit criticism of the way things are now, which some bosses don't want to hear.

There is an even more damaging aspect to this. If front-line staff hide market insights from their bosses, at least these first-level bosses are close to the market and in a good position to know what's going on. But then the first-level bosses also suppress and distort communication to their own bosses, who themselves do the same to their bosses, and so on up the hierarchy. The danger is that those with most power to set priorities and allocate resources have a perception of customer experience systematically biased towards the positive.

Reflecting on this filtering effect, Jack Welch, former chairman of GE, declared, *'Every layer is a bad layer. ... obstructing swift and simple communication ... We must create an atmosphere where people can speak up to somebody who can do something about their problem.'*[147]

Consider General Motors, arguably the most important company of the 20th century. Its collapse had many causes. One of these was its unwitting fostering of a culture of fear and denial which left it disconnected from customers, complacent about non-traditional competitors, and unable to learn and innovate at the required rate.

### *GM: 60 years of rejecting unwelcome messages*

In 1946, Peter Drucker published *The Concept of the Corporation* based on his detailed study of GM, which had commissioned the research. While most observers saw the book as strongly pro-GM and pro-business, GM itself saw it as *'An attack on the company, as hostile as any ever mounted by the left'*[148] and rejected all its recommendations.

For at least ten years, this arrogance appeared to be justified. In 1955, GM, Ford, and Chrysler sold 95% of the cars in North America, which itself represented 70% of the world market, with GM as the dominant player and by far the largest and most profitable industrial company in the world. From that point until it filed for bankruptcy in June 2009, however, it lost market share almost every year, mainly to non-US companies.

Yet since the 1920s GM has been a leading-edge market research practitioner. Drucker's 1946 book specifically praised its Customer Research group which *'intentionally, systematically and continuously supplies the customer's point of view to management, and which enables the designer, engineer, production man and salesman to see himself and his work as others see it'.*[149]

GM's strength in market research and analysis has continued. It has been a corporate member of the Marketing Science Institute since 1986. In 1991, its then Executive Director of Market Research and Planning, Vincent Barabba, co-authored with Gerald Zaltman, a leading marketing professor, *Hearing the Voice of the Market*, a highly-regarded book on *'competitive advantage through creative use of market information'*. At least in terms of formal market research, GM's ability to *generate* customer insights has always been world class.

But GM's track record of *listening to and acting on* customer insights has been dismal. Somewhere between its sophisticated market research and the products in the showroom, something has gone wrong for most of the last half century. The main reason, we believe, is GM's consistent failure to listen and respond to unwelcome messages about the market from both internal and external sources. It has had a culture which rejects unwelcome news, and its leaders have been unable or unwilling to change this. GM's indignant rejection of Drucker's 1946 book is just one example of its arrogant, non-listening culture. Here are more:

- Many GM alumni recall with anger and regret a climate that left top management detached from the realities of the market. One alumnus, a vice president in the 1990s, recalls how reports of quality problems on the line were so diluted as they went up the hierarchy that top management really did believe *'We don't have quality problems'*. Neither the reports they were receiving nor their own experience alerted them to the problem.
- In one encounter at the NUMMI plant, GM's joint venture with Toyota, managers met to review performance. One senior ex-GM manager reported 'no problems', only to be stopped by Katsuake Watanabe, then President of Toyota, and told, *'No problem is a problem'*.
- Brand guru Wally Olins, who has consulted for many car companies, told us, *'I found GM impossible to deal with. They had their own fixed ideas and always thought they were right.'*
- Another consultant who presented critical feedback on a proposed new product was cut short and sent back from Detroit on an earlier flight. The product flopped, as he'd predicted.

### *Your people aren't as open as you think*

GM may have been an extreme case (and we know there were many other factors) but fear and denial are widespread. Their impact is compounded by the routine, but largely unrecognized, 'spinning' of market feedback within organizations and a Pollyanna-ish view of how open we all are.

In one study, 180 executives from over 100 companies based in 25 countries told us that 'managing' information flows relating to market feedback was commonplace and detrimental. We asked them how they thought peers in their own companies would handle three different types of market feedback relating to: Customer Complaints, Market Research, and Business Development. In all three scenarios the market feedback was negative.[150]

If your working assumption is that when the market speaks your information channels work so that you hear the voice of the customer quickly and accurately, think again. 30% of respondents reckoned that their peers would not tell the truth about customer complaints *most of the time*. When the scenarios addressed market research findings and business development status, 20% and 30%, respectively, reckoned that their peers would not tell the truth most of the time.

Alarmed? We were. So, we discussed these findings with more executives, who confirmed that the grim picture was consistent with their reality. What we call 'truth telling' – the accurate and appropriate sharing of market insights – is anything but ubiquitous.

Because market signals are not getting through to those best placed to act on them, innovation is stifled. We asked the same respondents to rate their company's performance on an innovation scale. Surprise, surprise, companies that we judged to be more highly rated on truth telling were indeed more innovative, at least according to these self reports.

### *You're not as open as you think, either*

*Boss:* 'Why is Janet leaving?'
*Colleague:* 'She's been unhappy for months'
*Boss:* 'Why didn't she tell me?'
*Colleague:* 'She tried'.[151]

We also analyzed data from over 4 000 US managers across multiple industries and functions collected by Personnel Decisions International (PDI), a leader in 360-degree surveys. We found abundant evidence that, as a general rule, executives are far from open in practice, and also, that they are largely unaware of this. Relative to the opinions of their bosses, peers and subordinates, managers overestimate their own ability to listen to others' concerns.

Subordinates are far less convinced than their bosses are of the bosses' ability to encourage others to express their views. Most managers have inflated views of their openness, directness and willingness to listen. In contrast, the managers' bosses rate them significantly *higher* than they rate themselves on *'Listens to people without interrupting',* indicating the tendency of the bosses themselves to avoid interrupting their own bosses.

In 360-degree surveys, managers typically rate themselves higher on most competences than their colleagues do. But our research shows that the gap between managers' self evaluation and their colleagues' evaluation of them is widest of all when it comes to gauging receptiveness to difficult issues, as revealed by answers to statements such as '*Encourages others to express their views, even contrary ones*' and *'Listens willingly to concerns expressed by others'*.

The gap between managers' and colleagues' perception of the managers' openness to unwanted messages occurs, we believe, because, in most manager–subordinate relationships, the managers overestimate their openness to such messages *and* underestimate the extent to which the power difference discourages their subordinates from speaking up. Put simply, even good managers often unwittingly signal that they don't want to hear bad news (for instance by changing the subject or avoiding interaction) and subordinates tend to self-censor, avoiding delivering it.[152]

These misperceptions create a communication barrier, inhibiting the flow of bad, but useful, news (e.g. about quality problems or service failures) and sometimes even positive ideas for improvement, if the peer or subordinate feels that they might be perceived as criticism. How can you counter this natural tendency among both bosses and subordinates? First, let's look at an example.

When Sheryl Sandberg (now COO at Facebook) was a vice president at Google, her fiefdom included the company's crucial automated advertising system. She committed an error that cost Google several million dollars – *'Bad decision, moved too quickly, no controls in place, wasted some money,'* is all she'll say about it.

When she realized the scale of her mistake, she walked across the street to inform Larry Page, Google's cofounder and unofficial thought leader. *'I feel really bad about this,'* Sandberg told Page, who accepted her apology. But as she turned to leave, Page said something that surprised her. *'I'm so glad you made this mistake,'* he said. *'Because I want to run a company where we are moving too quickly and doing too much, not being too cautious and doing too little. If we don't have any of these mistakes, we're just not taking enough risk.'* [153]

Every top management says it wants people to take risks and communicate openly. But when a million-dollar mistake earns a pat on the back from the CEO, people start to believe it.

### *Opening up represents an underexploited opportunity*

The good news is that subordinates' fear represents a significant and surprisingly underexploited opportunity to boost customer focus, delivery, and innovation. Encouraging free and open communication of market information up the hierarchy can reap huge benefits:

- *Managers hear about both problems and ideas for improvement.* For instance, as we've discussed, customer complaints should be a source of learning and innovation – but only if they are communicated, analyzed, and followed up openly.
- *Managers get more honest feedback on their own ideas.* People nearer the customer are often better placed than their bosses to judge which proposed innovations are really relevant and will add value.
- *Implementation staff are more engaged and committed to successful execution and consistent quality.* Despite all the

> talk of empowerment and the motherhood statements in the annual report, engagement levels in most companies are low and possibly decreasing.

If you really want people to speak up about problems they encounter, you must create a workplace where they feel safe and encouraged to do so, even when the news isn't good. Unless you go out of your way to signal this consistently through your everyday actions, people will assume the opposite. Your first task is to acknowledge the problem and the opportunity, make openness an explicit value of the organization, and communicate it again and again through your actions as well as your words. The fear that stifles open communication up the hierarchy is a reflection of power differences, so reducing it has to start where the power is concentrated, at the top.

Recall the killer question for this chapter: *'Have front-line staff asked you any uncomfortable questions or suggested any important improvements over the last three months?'*. If the answer to this question is no, ask your HR team to find out why not. If they answer that staff do not feel able or comfortable in doing so, and are thus keeping silent, you need to act. Clear out whatever barriers have been erected between them and you, and encourage them to come forward.

You must also get the entire top management team to agree a clear vision and a set of values which include words such as openness, trust, respect, and collaboration as well as market and customer. Vividly communicate the vision and values, and always reflect them in your own actions: as well as fear, in most companies there is also widespread cynicism about top management statements and initiatives. As with parenting, what managers do matters more than what they say.

At another top Indian business group, Tata, this is an article of faith. Tata managers know they are judged by their customers and by the Indian public at large on what they do, not on what they say they are going to do. The idea of making a promise and not living up to it is entirely foreign to the Tata ethos and system of values.[154]

Creating a culture of openness is more about values than about techniques, but can be helped by rethinking customer and front-line contact programs and re-using 360° HR data for this purpose.

## Rethink Customer and Front-Line Contact Programs

The benefits of top managers meeting customers face to face, rather than relying only on market research and other second-hand knowledge, are so obvious that most firms now have formal customer contact programs. The value of these programs varies widely, however. In our research, we have found - to our surprise - that top managers in the most successful firms don't spend much more time with customers than managers in less successful firms. Instead, the main difference is in the nature of the contacts.

Managers from more successful companies didn't rate as helpful corporate entertainment, industry think-tanks, or highly structured and choreographed reviews with customers' senior executives. Instead, they focused on talking to customers informally on their own territory, seeing how they were doing, asking the tough questions and fearlessly getting the feedback that enabled improvement, spawned innovation, and built meaningful relationships.

Similar comments apply to top management contacts with the front line. Visiting a branch office for a couple of hours, like royalty, achieves almost nothing, especially if the visit is scheduled in advance: people will tell you that everything's great and what you take away will be both superficial and distorted. Instead, you need to spend enough time in each location you visit to learn what's really going on and what the issues are. One implication is that it may be better to visit just one branch office for several days or on several occasions than to drop in on several for a few hours each. Remember, the traditional tools of the anthropologist are the notebook, pencil, and suitcase: immersion applies at the front line as well as with the customer.

We've already mentioned the way successful B2B companies such as Research Now and Aggreko get close to their customers and also how managers in the best B2C firms such as P&G and Tesco supplement formal market research by getting personally immersed in the consumer market. Other examples we've encountered include top managers spending a day observing a salesman succeed and fail, scrubbing up to go into a hospital operating theater and see the company's medical equipment being used, and sitting down with a supplier's accountant to explain the company's paperwork.

Crucially, gaining coal-face insights first hand circumvents the filtering and distortion caused by fear and organizational politics. Further, by getting an up-to-date understanding of what is happening at the point of value creation, executives walk the talk and show their commitment to an open, learning, customer-focused culture. They are communicating that they really do want discussions about market performance to be frank.

Finally, first-hand anecdotal data, if backed up with hard data, can powerfully communicate to management the need to accept unwelcome ideas, as we now illustrate.

### *How the Tide brand team sold the radically new advertising strategy*

In Chapter 4, we described how the Tide brand team (both P&G and Saatchi & Saatchi) developed a radically different advertising strategy based on the insights they had gained from three weeks' immersion with consumers exploring the wider context of their time-pressured everyday lives. The team's next challenge was to sell the new strategy to P&G's top management, most of whom had worked on Tide at some point in the past. The new proposal was risky, as it required a contemporary understanding of the target consumer.

To help P&G's top management accept the risk of this proposal, the agency used the immersive research to achieve buy-in. Eschewing Powerpoint, the agency wrote a series of monologues using only verbatim quotations from the research and hired three actresses to perform them in a theatrical presentation at P&G's corporate headquarters in Cincinnati. All of P&G's top management was invited to the performance. The quotations powerfully communicated what mattered to the women the brand team had met, e.g.:

> 'The most important thing in my life right now is raising my children. Who they become will affect our whole family - forever. I long to hear my children say that they feel good about themselves.'
>
> 'I am single and live with my epileptic dog. The last time I cried was about a month ago when she had thirteen seizures in one night. The vet suggested I have her put to sleep. But I won't'.

At the end of the performance, the top management simply said, *'Just do it'*. The depth of consumer understanding communicated by the data, presented in this way, left no reasonable room for doubt.

Even in companies without P&G's resources, mid-level managers can still use these types of ethnographic data - verbatim quotes in reports, video clips from customer interviews - to communicate unwelcome insights and messages to their bosses. Of course, they will usually also need hard data to support the case, but it is often the ethnographic part that really makes the point. This approach can be especially powerful in a B2B context: if a successful partner in a professional service firm sees a video of a top client saying that his technical knowledge is great but he doesn't listen, he'll find it hard to deny the problem.

## Reuse 360° Data

Assuming you have good market sensing programs in place, you need to measure the efficiency and effectiveness of the information flow through the organization. Most companies have significant scope for improvement in this regard.

The place to start is by measuring how much the conditions in the different units, functions, and levels in your organization encourage people to suppress and distort market information. For obvious reasons, getting helpful data on this is difficult: the more fearful people are, the more likely they are to distort responses if asked directly. One solution is to use data from 360° surveys on managers' self perception of their openness to difficult input, relative to others' perceptions of them, as we discussed on pages 136–137. These data should be routinely monitored and discussed at the highest level with the same regularity as unit costs, customer feedback, innovation pipeline and days' inventory.

Where there is a large gap between managers' self perception and their peers' and subordinates' perceptions of the managers' openness to difficult messages, this should act as a flashing light showing the need and opportunity for improvement. This is similar to the way NPS and other customer satisfaction/dissatisfaction measures can be used to highlight a negative gap between customers' expectations and their actual experience of the brand or company, discussed in Chapter 3.

If you want to increase the company's openness, you must ensure that these measures are emphasized in appraisals, rewards, and promotions. You should especially stress the perceptions of the managers' behavior among their subordinates and, to a lesser extent, peers. Conversely, the key measures of managers' perceptions of their subordinates include the subordinates' willingness to raise difficult issues which might help drive innovation. Both are important and mutually reinforcing.

The good news is that you may well already be gathering the data for the direct benefit of the individual executive and the implied indirect benefit of the organization. Take the small additional step of looking at the organizational perspective in addition to that of the individual. Don't waste the opportunity to leverage these existing data at the organizational level.

**Idea Check**

Don't let people's fear of repercussions stifle innovation in your company. See where you stand today.

***1. Can a middle manager in your company clearly describe two or three iconic moments that represent a culture of openness?***

If they can't, you don't have an open culture. Do members of your management team routinely disagree with you, using customer data to support their view? No? You don't have an open culture.

***2. Do you have a formal process for encouraging, capturing, processing and adopting (or not) improvements?***

Every suggestion should be acknowledged and followed up, even if the final outcome is a message explaining why you will not be implementing it. Promote, reward, and celebrate people and, especially, teams that make great suggestions.

***3. How many of your encounters with customers offer improvement opportunities?***

Not many? Try harder. This is potentially the most useful feedback you can get. Focus especially on your most valuable and most dissatisfied customers. Lapsed customers, if you can reach them, can be even more useful - and you might even win some of them back.

***4. How often do you have high-quality interactions with front-line staff?***

These can be your fastest route to a valid, unmediated picture of customer realities as well as signalling that the company's values are for real. Don't let organizational protocols get in the way. You'll know that you are not feared and that quality information is flowing when front-liners build a rapport with senior managers and see it as their responsibility to be the business's market-sensing eyes and ears.

***5. Are you using 360-degree data on managers' openness to unwelcome messages?***

Make these a prominent feature of the appraisal and reward system. More broadly, use them for organizational development: which are the units and functions where there's a problem?

***6. Are you using customer dissatisfaction data routinely to drive improvement?***

We assume you've read Chapter 2 and are now collecting data on customer dissatisfaction and its drivers as well as on customer satisfaction. But have you created a culture where these data are *routinely* discussed openly and used to drive improvement? If not, you must try harder to communicate through your actions that the main aim is to improve the customer experience, not to find people to blame.

# POSTSCRIPT

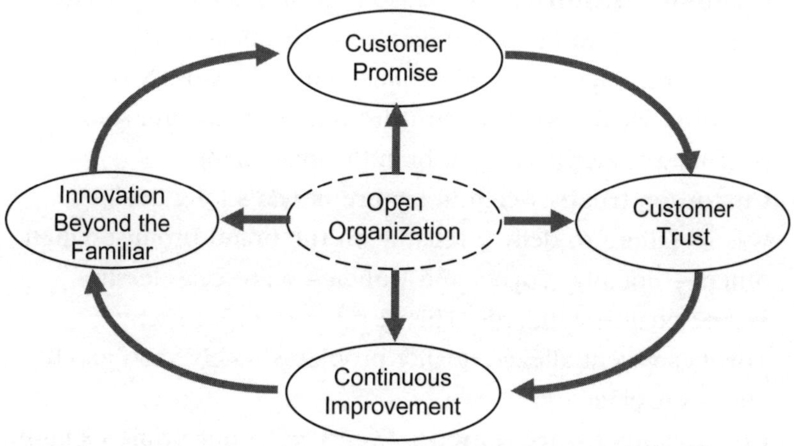


*'All happy families are alike; each unhappy family is unhappy in its own way'*

– Russian novelist Leo Tolstoy[155]

Tolstoy may have overstated the similarity of different happy families but his point was that unhappy families vary more. The same is true of successful and unsuccessful companies. Successful companies also vary enormously: IBM, Apple, P&G, Research Now, Aggreko, Infosys, Amex, Toyota and Best Buy are all very different. But the reason why our framework is generic is that what all these companies have in common - whether large or small, B2B or B2C, product- or service-based, premium-priced or value-based - is ambition and a clear, relevant brand promise which they communicate internally as well as to customers, reliably deliver, and relentlessly improve, all supported by a wide range of customer insights and an open organizational culture.

In contrast, like unhappy families, companies can malfunction for many reasons, including a failure to address any combination of one or more of the five sets of issues in the framework:

- **Customer promise:** One reason for Motorola's failure to maintain its lead in mobile handsets was its lack of a clear, consistent, relevant brand promise. In the 1980s, Nokia had the same weakness, but learnt from its mistake and soon became a leader in holistic brand management.
- **Customer trust:** A central feature of GM's long decline was its failure to deliver reliably on the brand promise when others - notably, Toyota and Honda - were ceaselessly raising quality standards. This also helps explain why Toyota's recent alleged quality problems received so much media coverage.
- **Continuous improvement:** Even P&G - our prime example of incremental innovation and customer focus in Chapter 4 - has sometimes faltered on this. In the late 1990s, it got distracted from improving its core products and brands and lost 40% of its market capitalization, only partly because Wall Street was mesmerized by the internet. An overemphasis on looking for breakthrough innovations made P&G forget the basics.[156] Again, the Tide advertising story discussed on pages 74–78 was about P&G playing catch-up with rapidly changing consumers.
- **Successful innovation:** Nokia's relatively slow and steady approach has made it vulnerable to fleet-footed new entrants such as Apple and Google who see mobile handsets mainly as

always-on handheld computers, not cell phones. Nokia is now working to become more adept at innovating beyond the familiar – as must Toyota in terms of corporate communications in the aggressive media, legal and political environment of the US and Europe.

- **Open organization:** GM was a clear example of a company in which unwanted messages failed to get through, but the other evidence in Chapter 6 shows that it is far from unique.

*What does this mean for you?*

The implication for you is clear. **Your first task is an honest, probably painful, evidence-based appraisal of where your organization or unit has most room to improve**. Remember the five 'killer questions' we first introduced in Chapter 1:

- Can your middle managers accurately describe your customer promise?
- Can all members of your senior executive team name the three things that most undermine trust among your existing customers?
- Is your brand really the best option for customers? Will it continue to be next month and next year?
- Have you embraced any novel ideas that have produced significant innovations beyond the familiar during the past year?
- Have front-line staff asked you any uncomfortable questions or suggested any important improvements to your offering during the last three months?

Of course these are only examples, but they illustrate the kinds of uncomfortable question you should be asking. You'll find others in the Idea Checks at the end of Chapters 2–6. Crucially, the five questions and the five sets of Idea Checks emphasize the need for evidence, both hard and soft: a running theme has been that the organizational barriers to long-term, market-driving organic profit growth often stem from the difference between the way things seem to be (to those with executive power) and the way they really are. Only data - hard and soft - can bridge that gap. In the words attributed to quality guru W. Edwards Deming, *'In God we trust: All others must bring data'.*

**The more weaknesses you can find, the more opportunities there will be to improve.** This self-critical diagnostic process will also help you prioritize your improvement program, focusing on the area(s) of greatest weakness, just as we have emphasized addressing the main drivers of customer *dis*satisfaction before turning to the drivers of satisfaction. This isn't easy. Our framework will help you structure the discussion you need to have with your colleagues, starting from wherever you are.

This is a journey, not an overnight transformation. Consider Philips's progress towards the kind of company described in this book.

### *The Philips marketing journey*

When Philips embraced a customer-focused organic growth strategy in 2002, it had to start from the very beginning. It developed a new brand promise: advanced, easy to use products and services designed around user needs. The positioning, with the strap-line *'Sense and Simplicity'*, reflects a deep understanding of most people's relationship with technology and addresses the main source of their frequent dissatisfaction with it.

*Sense and Simplicity* is, however, much more than a strap-line. It helps drive decision-making and standard-setting for internal as well as customer-facing processes. It guides planning and resourcing, acting as a beacon for progress and change. Customer satisfaction metrics are used meticulously to drive the improvement process. Since the launch of *Sense and Simplicity* in 2004, Philips's brand value has almost doubled from $4.4bn to $8.7bn, further strengthening its innovation capability.[157]

Like all organizational transformations, the Philips Marketing Journey began with an honest and painful recognition of where the company was and the resulting need for - in Philips's case - radical change in a proud company. Pride in achievement is good, but not when it becomes arrogance, complacency, or failure to listen to the voice of the customer. At Philips, it took pressure from the financial markets to force an initial self examination in the 1990s, and the crash of 2001 to create the sense of urgency needed to drive the full change process. This process has involved a sustained effort to move from a factory, technology and product mindset to a market mindset, led by the CEO and a newly appointed corporate CMO; a clear brand positioning (products and solutions that are designed around you, easy to use, and advanced); and a Marketing Academy and other HR and organizational initiatives to make it happen.

The Philips Marketing Journey - which still has some way to go - illustrates how successful leadership requires extreme persistence and occasional willingness to be unpopular. Keeping a business constantly improving ahead of the competition, ensuring that its products are always customer-relevant, driving changes in culture or established ways of doing things, avoiding complacency, staying agile and alert to shifts in markets and technologies - all this involves a never-ending effort by the leadership.

What companies need at the top is neither autocrats nor weak leaders, but *strong leaders who genuinely listen* to the evidence and arguments. Sometimes, having genuinely listened, they simply have to insist that something is done the way they want: there were two occasions when Gerard Kleisterlee, the Philips CEO, just put his foot down to overcome top management resistance and said, *'We're doing it'*. At some point, to achieve the necessary changes in your company or unit, you too will likely have to say the same.

### *It's up to you now*

In the preface, we made the bold claim - our own customer promise - that if you really treat this book as a call to action and follow it up, your business is almost certain to improve its long-term performance. We hope the evidence and arguments have persuaded you to take up that challenge. If so, it's up to you now.

www.beyond-the-familar.com

# END NOTES

1. Bala Chakravarthy and Peter Lorange, *Profit or Growth?: Why You Don't Have to Choose*, Philadelphia, Wharton School Publishing, 2007.
2. Patrick Barwise and Seán Meehan, *Simply Better: Winning and Keeping Customers by Delivering What Matters Most*, Boston: Harvard Business School Press, 2004 (winner of the American Marketing Association's 2005 Berry-AMA Book Prize).
3. Andrew Edgecliffe-Johnson and Tim Bradshaw, 'The adman cometh in pursuit of growth', *Financial Times*, June 30, 2008.
4. Ronald Henkoff, 'Keeping Motorola on a Roll', *Fortune*, April 18, 1994.
5. Liz Vaughan-Adams, 'Nokia extends lead over global rivals,' *The Independent*, January 06, 2001, http://www.independent.co.uk/news/business/news/nokia-extends-lead-over-global-rivals-705458.html
6. Matt Richtel, 'Will the Handset Spinoff Really Help Motorola?' *New York Times*, May 1, 2009.
7. 'Gartner Says Worldwide Mobile Device Sales Grew 13.8 Percent in Second Quarter of 2010, But Competition Drove Prices Down,' August 12, 2010. http://www.gartner.com accessed September 18, 2010.
8. Nokia Corporation 'Towards Telecommunications Nokia Publication,' August 2000, http://www.nokia.com/NOKIA_COM_1/About_Nokia/Sidebars_new_concept/Broschures/TowardsTelecomms.pdf.

Nokia Corporation 'History of Nokia,' 2001, http://www.fundinguniverse.com/company-histories/Nokia-Corporation-Company-History.html.

9. Martti Haikio, *Nokia - The Inside Story*, (Helsinki: Edita, 2002), 149. Nokia Annual Report, 1997.
10. Sydney Finkelstein and Shade H. Sandford, 'The Rise and Fall of Iridium', *Organizational Dynamics*, 29, 2 (November 2000), 138-148.
11. Dan Steinbock, *The Nokia Revolution*, (AMACOM, 2001), 279-283; Martti Haikio, *Nokia - The Inside Story*, (Helsinki: Edita, 2002), 134-137.
12. Interbrand, 'Best global brands 2000'. Interbrand. Even today (September 2010) Nokia is, perhaps controversially, still ranked #8 in Interbrand's valuations - well above Apple at#17.
13. While Nokia was experiencing a downturn, Motorola and Ericsson both experienced increased profits despite the change in market circumstances. Nokia suffered worst because it was the least vertically integrated. Carlos Cordon, Tom Vollmann and Jussi Heikkila, *Nokia Mobile Phones (A): Supply Chain Management*, IMD case IMD-6-0197, published 1997.
14. Kari-Pekka Wilska, president of Nokia Americas, cited in Haikio (2001), p 203.
15. Motorola, 'A Timeline Overview of Motorola History 1928-2008,' 2008, http://www.motorola.com/mot/doc/6/6800_MotDoc.pdf. Motorola, 'A Timeline of Motorola Milestones and Innovations,' June 11, 2003, http://www.motorola.com/mot/doc/0/613_MotDoc.pdf
16. Nancy Gohring, 'Motorola's goal: Be boring,' *Info World*, September 05,2007,http://www.infoworld.com/article/07/09/05/Motorolas-goal-is-to-be-boring_1.html
17. Andy Reinhardt, 'Nokia: Suddenly, It's Sweating,' *Business Week*, June 23, 2003, http://www.businessweek.com/magazine/content/03_25/b3838644.htm
18. Dan Steinbock, *The Nokia Revolution*, (AMACOM, 2001), 135.
19. Gary F. Gebhardt, Gregory S. Carpenter, and John F. Sherry Jr., 'Creating a Market Orientation: A Longitudinal, Multi-Firm, Grounded

Analysis of Cultural Transformation', *Journal of Marketing*, 70, 4, October 2006, 37-54.

20. Web postings from existing and former employees in 2008 include the following comments:

    'Most managers are overwhelmed, underpowered, poorly informed and narrowly focused. Managers like to score points for making decisions - cancelling features, cancelling products, taking short-cuts ... I've never worked at a place where individuals' contributions were so wantonly wasted ... Few are on the same page.' (exMotoDesigner - posted 9 Mar 08).

    An existing employee says: 'Motorola is a great company with I'm sorry to say lousy leaders'. (Motorolan - posted 30 Jan 08).

    And an ex-employee says: 'I left Motorola after a single, dreadful year in the back-stabbing toxic culture described above ... 3 years ago the problems so apparent today were obvious then: weak, dog's breakfast of a product line, little 3G effort, failing brand equity, irrational pricing and a process that virtually assured a mediocre product.' (ex-Motorolan, posted 30 Jan 08).

    And another: 'I used to work for Symbol Technologies and loved it: great company, great products, and decent management. When Motorola acquired the company, it was time to go: Motorola has the most horrible work environment I have ever encountered: back-stabbing, silos, no employee empowerment - they are stuck in the 80s from a (sic) employee management perspective.' (Anonymous, posted 30 Jan 08).

21. Lots of examples given in the *Business Week* article (July 16, 2001), for instance the Shark phone launched to low-end European market in the mid-late nineties. Motorola's own market data indicated that consumers were already preferring competitors' phones which were smaller at comparable prices. Yet the launch went ahead and the product bombed in Europe.

22. Roger O. Crockett, 'Motorola, Can Chris Galvin save his family's legacy,' *Business Week*, July 16, 2001, http://www.businessweek.com/magazine/content/01_29/b3741001.htm

23. Kevin O'Brien, 'Nokia's new Chief Faces Culture of Complacency,' *New York Times*, September 20, 2010.

24. Indeed, some analysts argue that Apple's stock, currently riding high, flatters. See Scott Cendrowski, 'Should you Buy Apple Stock?' *Fortune*, September 27, 2010 p21.
25. According to Booz, Allen and Hamilton, and Forbes, 40% of new products fail in the market. Golder and Tellis put this figure at 47%. George Day's 2006 MSI analysis of risk-reward of an innovation that is new to the company both in terms of technology and in terms of the market, gives an 85–95% probability of failure of such a venture.
26. George Orwell, *Animal Farm* (Secker and Warburg, 1945), 51.
27. Constantinos C. Markides and Paul A. Geroski, *Fast Second: How Smart Companies Bypass Radical Innovation to Enter and Dominate New Markets*, Jossey-Bass, 2005.
28. Based on Patrick Barwise and Seán Meehan, 'Is Your Company as Customer-Focused As You Think?' *MIT Sloan Management Review*, 51, 3 (Spring 2010), 63–68.
29. www.allaboutbranding.com
30. Patrick Barwise and Colin Strong, 'Permission-based mobile advertising', *Journal of Interactive Marketing* 16, 1 (2002), 14–24. Patrick Barwise was an early investor in TMC and a member of its advisory panel. He no longer has a financial interest or other involvement in the company.
31. £1000 invested when TMC was first set up in April 2000 would have been worth £65 000 at the time of the IPO in August 2005 and £240 000 by the time of the e-Rewards acquisition in December 2009.
32. The other main meaning is as a representation of a company, as in '*Brand Bullies*' in the subtitle of Naomi Klein's 2001 best-seller *No Logo.* This treats brands as symbols of companies of which Ms Klein disapproves.
33. Jeremy Bullmore, *Apples, Insights and Mad Inventors: An Entertaining Analysis of Modern Marketing* (John Wiley & Sons, Ltd, Chichester, England: 2006), 67.
34. At the same time, because brand equity exists only in customers' heads, it does not belong to the company. Trademarks do belong to the company and can be bought and sold – and even stolen, if not

well protected - like other assets. But a 'bare' trademark with no associated brand equity has little if any value. This is one reason why brand valuations remain controversial and the financial reporting rules impose tight limits on their recognition in company balance sheets. See Patrick Barwise, Chris Higson, Andrew Likierman, and Paul Marsh, *Accounting for Brands*, London: Institute of Chartered Accountants in England and Wales, 1989.

35. Hermann Simon, *Hidden Champions: Lessons from 500 of the World's best Unknown Companies*, Boston, MA: Harvard Business School Press, 1996.
36. This is a slight overgeneralization. A brand whose customer acquisition model is entirely based on either direct marketing or peer-to-peer introductions can grow without high brand awareness within the target market, although a strong brand will always help. Research Now's B2C brand Valued Opinions is an example of the first type. An exclusive membership club would be an example of the second.
37. We provide a general framework for marketing communications planning in Chapter 5 of *Simply Better*.
38. Richard T. Pascale, 'Perspectives on Strategy: The Real Story Behind Honda's Success', *Californian Management Review*, Volume XXVI No3. Spring 1984, 55.
39. Interview with co-founder Dan Lee, February 5, 2009. In 2010, the company repurchased News International's stake and then sold it to DMGT, the second largest national newspaper group (Mark Sweney, 'DMGT acquires 50% stake in Globrix' (www.guardian.co.uk/media/2010/jan/21/dmgt-globrix).
40. This is a big topic in its own right, well covered in other books such as *The Anatomy of Buzz: How to Create Word Of Mouth Marketing* by Emanuel Rosen, Broadway Business (2002), *The Anatomy of Buzz Revisited: Real-Life Lessons in Word-of-Mouth Marketing*, by Emanuel Rosen, Broadway Business (2009), *Inbound Marketing: Get Found Using Google, Social Media, and Blogs (The New Rules of Social Media)* by Brian Halligan, Dharmesh Shah and David Meerman-Scott, Wiley (2009). First though, Malcolm Gladwell's *The Tipping Point* (Back Bay Books, 2002) is a must-read. We here review the issues only briefly.

41. Rex Crum, 'Apple buzz reaches high point on eve of tablet debut,' *Market Watch*, January 27, 2010.
42. 'Market Watch: Global Round-up', *Datamonitor*, September 2005, 73.
43. Amy Gilroy, 'JVC Launches Viral Ad,' *TWICE: This Week in Consumer Electronics*, June 2, 2008, 58.
44. Gary Silverman, *Financial Times*, September 16, 2004, 14.
45. Patrick Barwise and Seán Meehan, *Simply Better: Winning and Keeping Customers by Delivering What Matters Most* (Boston: Harvard Business School Press, 2004, page x). 'Brand' in this quotation refers to a specific named product or service. The research evidence behind it is spelt out in Chapter 2 of *Simply Better*.
46. Barwise and Meehan (2004), *Simply Better* op cit, Chapter 5.
47. From his poem 'To a Louse'.
48. Erika Askeland, 'Saturday Profile: Rupert Soames,' *Scotsman*, June 21, 2008, http://thescotsman.scotsman.com/management/Saturday-profile-Rupert-Soames.4209467.jp'
49. Erika Askeland, 'Saturday Profile: Rupert Soames," *Scotsman*, June 21, 2008, http://thescotsman.scotsman.com/management/Saturday-profile-Rupert-Soames.4209467.jp'
50. Frederick F. Reichheld, 'The one number you need to grow,' *Harvard Business Review*, December 2003.
51. When the ATM was invented is the subject of some debate. The ATM was first conceptualized by Luther George Simjian in 1939. He persuaded what is now Citicorp to try it. After six months, the bank abandoned the project having reported that the only people using the machines were a small number of prostitutes and gamblers who didn't want to deal with tellers face to face. http://web.mit.edu/invent/iow/simjian.html. The ATM as we know it today was launched in 1969. It is generally considered to be the brainchild of Don Wenzel who first imagined it when standing for too long in a queue for a bank teller in Houston, Texas. http://www.thocp.net/hardware/atm.htm
52. Joseph B. Myers, Andrew D. Pickersgill, and Evan S. Van Metre, 'Steering customers to the right channels,' *McKinsey Quarterly*, November 2004.

53. '"Thank you for calling NTL ... now f*** off,"' *Daily Telegraph*, September 27, 2004, http://www.telegraph.co.uk/news/1472746/Thank-you-for-calling-NTL...now-f-off.html
54. Timothy L. Keiningham, Bruce Cooil, Tor Wallin Andreassen, and Lerzan Aksoy, 'A Longitudinal Examination of Net Promoter and Firm Revenue Growth', *Journal of Marketing*, 71 (July 2007): 39–51.
55. www.theacsi.org
56. Rhymer Rigby, 'Bosses hang out at fast-food joints for invaluable tips', *Financial Times* (UK edition), February 17, 2009, 12.
57. Accenture Global Customer Satisfaction Study 2007, 'Customer satisfaction in the changing global economy,' 2007, http://www.accenture.com/Global/Consulting/Customer_Relationship_Mgmt/R_and_I/AccentureSurvey.htm
58. Amy Barrett, 'When, Why and How to fire that Customer', *Business Week*, November, 2007, http://www.businessweek.com/magazine/content/07_44/b4056431.htm
59. David Twiddy, 'Sprint Nextel defends decision to terminate customers who call customer service too much', *AP newswire*, July 10, 2007.
60. Professor Claes Fornell and Stephen M. Ross, 'First Quarter of 2008', May 20, 2008 http://www.theacsi.org/index.php?option=com_content&task=view&id=179&Itemid=182
61. Marguerite Reardon, 'Sprint breaks up with high-maintenance customers', July 5, 2007, http://news.cnet.com/8301-10784_3-9739869-7.html?tag=mncol.
62. www.theacsi.org accessed on October 7, 2010.
63. Teresa F. Lindeman, 'Sometimes they are more bother than they are worth', *Knight-Ridder Tribune Business News*, July 11, 2007.
64. www.theacsi.org accessed on October 7, 2010.
65. It is unclear whether Edison ever spoke these widely cited words but they certainly reflect his approach. For instance, in seeking to tap the huge market potential for high-quality recorded sound, he rejected initial solutions saying the cylinders were too expensive, took too long to produce, and were of insufficient quality. He felt that there had to be a better way and set out to

find it. See: André J Millard, *America on Record: A History of Recorded Sound*, New York: Cambridge University Press, 1995, page 44.

66. Judah Ginsberg, *The Development of Tide*, American Chemical Society, 2006, http://portal.acs.org/portal/acs/corg/content?_nfpb=true&_pageLabel=PP_ARTICLEMAIN&node_id=929&content_id=CTP_004463&use_sec=true&sec_url_var=region1
67. Davis Dyer, Frederick Dalzell and Rowena Olegario, '*Rising Tide: Lessons from 165 Years of Brand Building at Procter & Gamble*', (Boston: Harvard Business School Press, 2004), 67.
68. Judah Ginsberg, *The development of Tide*.
69. Judah Ginsberg, *The development of Tide*.
70. A.G. Lafley and Ram Charan, '*Game-Changer: How You Can Drive Revenue and Profit Growth with Innovation*', (New York: Crown Business, 2008), 82.
71. Davis Dyer, Frederick Dalzell and Rowena Olegario, '*Rising Tide: Lessons from 165 Years of Brand Building at Procter & Gamble*', (Boston: Harvard Business School Press, 2004), 80.
72. Roger L. Martin, '*The Opposable Mind*', (Harvard Business School Press, 2007), 173–176.
73. John Pepper, *What Really Matters*, (Bantam Books, 2005), 91.
74. A.G. Lafley and Ram Charan, '*Game-Changer: How You Can Drive Revenue and Profit Growth with Innovation*' (New York: Crown Business, 2008), 80.
75. Effie awards 2007, 'Tide Knows Fabrics Best' campaign. http://www.effie.org/winners/showcase/2007/1675
76. A.G. Lafley and Ram Charan, '*Game-Changer: How You Can Drive Revenue and Profit Growth with Innovation*', (New York: Crown Business, 2008), 82.
77. In the five years since 1996, Tide's annual household penetration (the proportion of US households buying it at least once in the year) had fallen from 43.9% to 37.8%. These and other data are from P&G and Saatchi and Saatchi.
78. Tide's value share increased from 37.4% to 43.2% between 2001 to 2005. (Data from Saatchi and Saatchi).

79. A.G. Lafley and Ram Charan, '*Game-Changer: How You Can Drive Revenue and Profit Growth with Innovation*', (New York: Crown Business, 2008), 4.
80. Gerald Zaltman, and R. Coulter. 'Seeing the Voice of the Customer: Metaphor-based Advertising Research'. *Journal of Advertising Research* 35, no. 4 (July-August 1995): 35-51.
81. Carol Berning, Interview with the author, July 31, 2006.
82. A.G. Lafley and Ram Charan, '*Game-Changer: How You Can Drive Revenue and Profit Growth with Innovation*', (New York: Crown Business, 2008), 34. J.P. Donlon, 'Lafley's Law: If You Want to Win Become a Game-Changer', *Chief Executive-* Articles/Archives, July 23, 2008, http://www.chiefexecutive.net/ME2/Audiences/dirmod.asp?sid=&nm=&type=Publishing&mod=Publications%3A%3AArticle&mid=8F3A7027421841978F18BE895F87F791&tier=4&id=8B79F0D0B7394691B7F544FF938DAB76&AudID=ae720e7de3fe473693930869a5157c27
83. A.G. Lafley and Ram Charan, '*Game-Changer: How You Can Drive Revenue and Profit Growth with Innovation*', (New York: Crown Business, 2008), 38, 43, 48.
84. Carol Berning, Interview with the author, July 31, 2006.
85. Carol Berning, Interview with the author, July 31, 2006.
86. Household penetration declined from 37.8% in 2001 to 33.6% in 2005. (Figures from Saatchi and Saatchi).
87. Wanda Pogue (Saatchi and Saatchi, NYC), Interview with the author, August 7, 2006.
88. Wanda Pogue (Saatchi and Saatchi, NYC), Interview with the author, August 7, 2006.
89. Kevin Roberts, 'Beyond the horizon', Kevin Roberts web page, April 24, 2008, http://www.saatchikevin.com/Beyond_the_Horizon/
90. Robert Berner, 'Detergent Can Be So Much More - P&G's new ads strive to "stake out the emotional high ground"', *Business Week*, May 1, 2006, http://www.businessweek.com/magazine/content/06_18/b3982087.htm
91. Patrick Barwise and Seán Meehan, *Simply Better*, (Harvard Business School Press, 2004), 171-177.

92. Tony Friscia, 'A Conversation with Procter & Gamble CEO A.G. Lafley,' *AMR Research*, April 18, 2008, http://www.amrresearch.com/content/View.asp?pmillid=21388
93. David A. Aaker, *Managing Brand Equity*, (Maxwell Macmillan International, 1991), 5-6.
94. Procter & Gamble website, 'Procter and Gamble Solutions', 2009 http://www.pgbrands.com/Default.aspx?tabid=92
95. Clive Humby, Terry Hunt, and Tim Phillips, *Scoring Points: How Tesco Continues to Win Customer Loyalty*, London and Philadelphia, PA: Kogan Page, second edition, 2007.
96. Eric von Hippel, *Democratizing Innovation*, Cambridge, MA: MIT Press, 2006.
97. Jonathan Alan Silver and John Charles Thompson, *Understanding Customer Needs: A Systematic Approach to the 'Voice of the Customer'*, Master's Thesis, Sloan School of Management, Cambridge, MA: MIT, June 1991.
98. This discussion draws on Patrick Barwise and Seán Meehan, 'The One Thing You Must Get Right When Building a Brand', *Harvard Business Review*, December 2010.
99. Tim Brown, 'Thinking', *Harvard Business Review*, June 2008, 85-92. Tim Brown is CEO of the Palo Alto-based innovation and design consultancy IDEO. This article is about 'thinking like a designer' and covers a range of issues including fast prototyping.
100. Jena McGregor, 'The World's Most Innovative Companies', *Business Week*, May 4, 2007, http://www.businessweek.com/innovate/content/may2007/id20070504_051674.htm.
101. Michael Arndt and Bruce Einhorn, The 50 Most Innovative Companies, *Bloomberg Businessweek* April 15, 2010: www.businessweek.com/magazine/content/10_17/b4175034779697.htm.
102. Connie Guglielmo and Dina Bass, Apple overtakes Microsoft in market capitalization, Businessweek.com May 26, 2010, accessed September 8, 2010.
103. Claes Fornell, 'ACSI Commentary September 2010'. http://www.theacsi.org/index.php?option=com_content&task=view&id=222&Itemid=240

104. PARC invented many of these technologies itself and combined them with others invented elsewhere. For instance, the computer mouse was patented in 1967 by the Stanford Research Institute, which subsequently licensed the idea to Apple for a nominal sum. Peter Forbes, 'Douglas Engelbart demonstrates the first computer mouse, December 1967', *FT Magazine*, April 10, 2010, page 46 (www.definingmoment@ft.com)
105. Technically, 'Star' refers to the office automation software sold with the product, which was officially the Xerox 8010 Information System.
106. Robert X. Cringely, 'The Television Program Transcripts: Part III', June 1996, http://www.pbs.org/nerds/part3.html.
107. Leander Kahney, 'Apple: It's all about the brand', *Wired*, December 4, 2002.
108. Jessica Ravitz, 'Apple fans mark 25 years of Mac devotion', CNN .com, http://edition.cnn.com/2009/TECH/01/23/apple.macintosh .anniversary/index.html Accessed on Jan 23 2007.
109. Apple Corporation, United States Securities and Exchange Commission (USSEC) form 10K, for the fiscal year ending September 26, 2010, (Washington D.C: 20549, October 27, 2010).
110. Peter Burrows, 'The Seed of Apple's innovations', *Business Week*, October 12, 2004, http://www.businessweek.com/bwdaily/dnflash/oct2004/nf20041012_4018_db083.htm.
111. Betsy Morris, 'What makes Apple Golden', *Fortune*, March 3, 2008, http://money.cnn.com/2008/02/29/news/companies/amac_apple .fortune/index.htm.
112. Harvard guru Clayton Christensen, in his landmark work on disruptive innovations, uses the example of the Newton to argue against 'all-or-nothing' bets. He advises innovators to '*conserve resources to get it right on the second or third try*'. See Clayton Christensen, *The Innovator's Dilemma: When New Technologies Cause Great Firms to Fail*, (Harvard Business School Press, 1997), 139.
113. In this context, Apple's most unusual feature is its extreme secrecy and – relatedly – its limited use of formal market research.
114. George S. Day, *Closing the Growth Gap: Balancing 'Big I' and 'small I' Innovation*, MSI working paper 06-004 (2006), Cambridge MA: Marketing Science Institute, pages 4–5.

115. George S. Day and Paul J. H. Shoemaker, 'Scanning the Periphery', *Harvard Business Review*, November 2005, 135–148.
116. Eric Von Hippel, 'Successful Industrial Products from Customer ideas,' *Journal of Marketing* January 1978, 39–49. Eric Von Hippel, 'Lead Users: A source of novel Product Concepts,' *Management Science* 32, no.7, (July 1986), 791-805.
117. Gary L. Lilien, Pamela D. Morrison, Kathleen Searls, Mary Sonnack and Eric von Hippel, 'Performance Assessment of the Lead User Idea Generation Process for New Product Development,' *Management Science*, 48, 8, August 2002, 1042–1059.
118. Bridget Angear and Miranda Sambles, 'How Walkers used co-creation to get the UK to do it a flavour', *Admap*, September 2009, 31–33.
119. Larry Huston and Nabil Sakkab, 'Connect and Develop: Inside Procter & Gamble's New Model for Innovation', *Harvard Business Review*, March 2006.
120. Open source innovation is not a new idea. In 1714, long before Wikinomics entered the vernacular, in an effort to enhance oceanic navigation, the British Government offered a prize to anyone who could measure longitude to within 60 nautical miles. It distributed around $150 000 to clockmakers and astronomers who had achieved the important breakthrough. Today companies such as Lego, Nike and Stata all harness the power of many customers to design, refine and improve their products in variants of the Longitude competition.
121. Patrick Barwise and Seán Meehan, *Simply Better: Winning and Keeping Customers by Delivering What Matters Most*, Boston, MA: Harvard Business School Press, 2004, 79–80.
122. Also a question of perspective. A salesperson trying a completely different approach to her sales pitches or her management of existing accounts would rightly see this as a radical innovation in terms of thinking process, risk, and potential return. But to her CEO, these changes would be so incremental that they wouldn't even appear on the radar.
123. George S. Day, *Closing the Growth Gap: Balancing 'Big I' and 'small I' Innovation*, MSI working paper 06-004 (2006), Cambridge MA: Marketing Science Institute, pages 5–6.

124. Personal correspondence with authors September 25, 2010, including Figure 5.1.
125. Beth Comstock, Ranjay Gulati and Stephen Liguori, 'Unleashing the Power of Marketing', *Harvard Business Review*, October 2010, 90–98.
126. Jean-Noel Kapferer and Vincent Bastien, *The Luxury Brand Strategy*, London and Philadelphia: Kogan Page, 2009, Chapter 7.
127. David A. Aaker and Kevin L. Keller, 'Consumer Evaluations of Brand Extensions', *Journal of Marketing* 54 (1990): 27–41. There is an extensive research literature on brand extensions, mostly from the 1990s. See Kevin Lane Keller, *Strategic Brand Management*, Upper Saddle River, NJ: Pearson Prentice Hall, third edition 2008, Chapter 12.
128. C. Whan Park, Sandra Milberg, and Robert Lawson, 'Evaluation of Brand Extensions: The Role of Product Feature Similarity and Brand Concept Consistency', *Journal of Consumer Research* 18 (1991): 185–193.
129. David A. Aaker, 'Brand Extensions: The Good, the Bad, and the Ugly', *Sloan Management Review* 31, 4 (1990), 47–56.
130. Matt Haig, *Brand Failures*, London and Sterling, VA: Kogan Page, 2003, 50–52.
131. Robert Smith 'Main Features in Management Information Systems', article click, 15 March 2008, http://www.articleclick.com/Article/Main-Features-in-Management-Information-Systems/980141.
132. L.C. Huff and W.T. Robinson (1994), 'The impact of lead time and years of competitive rivalry or pioneer market share advantage', *Management Science*, 40, 10, pp 1370–77. D. Szymanski, L. Troy and S. Bharadwaj (1995), Order of Entry and Business Performance: An Empirical Synthesis and Reexamination, *Journal of Marketing*, 59, 4 (October), pp 17–33.
133. Gerard J. Tellis and Peter N. Golder, 'First to Market, First to Fail? Real Causes of Enduring market Leadership', *MIT Sloan Management Review*, Vol. 37, No. 2, pp. 65–75, 1996, http://ssrn.com/abstract=906021. Peter N. Golder and Gerard J. Tellis, 'Pioneer Advantage: Marketing Logic or Marketing Legend?' *Journal of Marketing Research* 30, 2 (May 1993), 158–170.

134. Stephen P. Schnaars, *Managing Imitation Strategies: How Later Entrants Seize Markets from Pioneers*, New York: Free Press, 1994.
135. Constantinos C. Markides and Paul A. Geroski, *Fast Second: How Smart Companies Bypass Radical Innovation to Enter and Dominate New Markets*, San Francisco: Jossey-Bass, 2005.
136. W. Chan Kim and Renée Maubourgne, *Blue Ocean Strategy: How to Create Uncontested Market Space and Make the Competition Irrelevant*, (Harvard Business School Press, 2005).
137. To support their argument, Kim and Maubourgne include three case studies of long-term industry evolution and a paragraph and bar chart in Chapter 1 (pages 7–8) summarizing a study of the relative profitability of 'blue ocean' versus 'red ocean' strategies. In this study, the authors asked managers, after the event, about the revenue and profit impact of business launches. These were split into line extensions ('*incremental improvements within the red ocean of existing market space*') and launches '*aimed at creating blue oceans*'. Using these measures, only 14% of the launches fell into the 'blue ocean' category but these accounted for 38% of the resulting revenue growth and 61% of the profit growth. However, the study makes no allowance for the higher costs and much higher risks of 'blue ocean' launches versus 'red ocean' line extensions. It also suffers from so-called 'hindsight bias' – managers' perception that, if the project was successful, it must have been a radical pioneering breakthrough.
138. John Battelle, *The Search*, London and Boston, MA: Nicholas Brealey, 2005.
139. Reylito A. H. Elbo, *Business World*, March 6, 1996: 20.
140. Based on company sources including management interviews in Bangalore in March 2009.
141. Mitu Jayashankar and Shishir Prasad, 'Remaking INFY', *Business World*, September 22, 2003.
142. www.infosys.com
143. Case – Infosys Technologies; Prof Ashish Nanda, Thomas DeLong; Harvard Business School; May 23, 2002.
144. 'Infosys tops client satisfaction in outsourcing report', Infosys Press Release.

145. Kathleen M. Eisenhardt, Jean L. Kahwajy, and L.J. Bourgeois III, 'Taming Interpersonal Conflict in Strategic Choice: How Top Management Teams Argue, But Still Get Along,' in *Strategic Decisions*, ed. Vasilis Papadakis and Patrick Barwise (Norwell, M.A. Kluwer, 1997), 65–83. See Patrick Barwise and Seán Meehan, *Simply Better*, 164–5.
146. David Aaker, *Spanning Silos: The New CMO Imperative* (Boston: Harvard Business Press, 2008).
147. Robert Slater, *Jack Welch on Leadership* (New York: McGraw-Hill, 2004, p 67).
148. Peter Ferdinand Drucker, '*The Concept of the Corporation*,' Revised edition, (Transaction Publishers, 1993), Epilogue page 291.
149. Peter Ferdinand Drucker, '*The Concept of the Corporation*,' Revised edition, (Transaction Publishers, 1993), 93.
150. Willem Smit, and Seán Meehan (2009) '*True or false? A study of falsehoods in market intelligence dissemination?*' Best Paper in the Marketing Strategy Track, AMS Conference 2009, Academy of Marketing Science, Baltimore, MD, United States of America, May 20–23, 2009.
151. Patrick Barwise and Seán Meehan, 'So You Think You're a Good Listener', *Harvard Business Review*, April 2008, page 22.
152. There is an extensive literature on the role of fear and self-censorship in organizations. Studies include: J.C. Athanassiades, 'The Distortion of Upward Communication in Hierarchical Organizations', *Academy of Management Journal* 16, (1973) 207–226; M.J. Glauser, 'Upward Information Flow in Organizations: Review and Conceptual Analysis', *Human Relations* 37, 8 (1984) 613–643; J.E. Dutton, S.J. Ashford, R.M. O'Neill, E. Hayes and E.E. Wierba, 'Reading the Wind: How Middle Managers Assess the Context for Selling Issues to Top Managers', *Strategic Management Journal* 18, 5 (1997) 407–423; E.W. Morrison and F.J. Milliken, 'Organizational Silence: A Barrier to Change and Development in a Pluralistic World' *Academy of Management Review* 25, 4 (October 2000) 706–725; J.R. Detert and A.C. Edmondson, 'Why Employees Are Afraid to Speak', *Harvard Business Review* 85 (May 2007) 23–25.
153. Adam Lashinsky 'Chaos by Design,' *Fortune*, October 2, 2006.

154. Morgen Witzel, *Tata: The Evolution of a Corporate Brand*, Penguin Portfolio, 2010, especially Chapter 1, 'From Values to Value'.
155. Leo Tolstoy, *Anna Karenina*, translated by Richard Pevear and Larissa Volokhonsky, London: Penguin, 2000, page 1.
156. *Simply Better*, pages 171–6.
157. Interbrand, Best Global Brands 2004, 2010. www.thebestglobalbrands.com.

# INDEX

*Index compiled by Sophia Clapham*

# About the Authors

**Patrick Barwise** is emeritus professor of management and marketing at London Business School and chairman of Which?, the UK's leading consumer organization. He joined LBS in 1976 after an early career at IBM and has published widely on management, marketing, media, and research methods. He is an experienced conference speaker and expert witness, having worked on commercial, tax, and competition cases in Brussels, Frankfurt, London, Paris and Washington. He has also has been involved in two successful start-up businesses: the online field research company Research Now (acquired by e-Rewards in 2009) and the online brand community specialist Verve.

**Seán Meehan** is the Martin Hilti Professor of Marketing and Change Management at IMD in Lausanne, Switzerland. Since joining IMD in 1997, he has directed both its MBA program and its Orchestrating Winning Performance open executive program, but his main focus has been on designing and delivering customized offerings for leading global companies such as Air France-KLM, Caterpillar, Hilti, Mastercard, Sandvik, Telefonica, and Toyota. His research is about understanding and addressing the challenges of becoming customer-focused. His early career was in client service and marketing roles at Arthur Andersen and Deloitte.

The authors' previous book, *Simply Better: Winning and Keeping Customers by Delivering What Matters Most*, won the American Marketing Association's 2005 Berry-AMA Book Prize and has been translated into seven other languages. Their research has also been published in the *Harvard Business Review, MIT Sloan Management Review*, and other leading management journals.